Frank Henderson

Six Years in the Prisons of England

Frank Henderson

Six Years in the Prisons of England

ISBN/EAN: 9783744759847

Printed in Europe, USA, Canada, Australia, Japan

Cover: Foto ©ninafisch / pixelio.de

More available books at **www.hansebooks.com**

SIX YEARS

IN THE

PRISONS OF ENGLAND.

BY

A MERCHANT.

EDITED BY FRANK HENDERSON.

:PRINTED FROM " THE TEMPLE BAR MAGAZINE."

LONDON:
RICHARD BENTLEY, NEW BURLINGTON STREET.
Publisher in Ordinary to Her Majesty.
1869.

TO A

KIND AND DEVOTED BROTHER,

WHO CHEERED ME WITH WORDS OF

CHRISTIAN SYMPATHY AND BROTHERLY LOVE

DURING THE

DARKEST AND MOST DESOLATE HOURS

OF MY

PAST UNHAPPY CAREER,

THE FOLLOWING PAGES ARE AFFECTIONATELY INSCRIBED BY

THE AUTHOR.

CONTENTS.

— *Contents.* — vii

CHAPTER I.

MY COMMERCIAL ANTECEDENTS—HOW I GOT INTO PRISON.

IN the beginning of the year 1856 I commenced business on my own account, as a merchant in a Northern City. Previous to that time I had been engaged in an unsuccessful partnership, but I paid my creditors in full with the small capital advanced to me by my friends for the purpose of my new adventure. When I began operations, therefore, I was literally without a shilling in the world, but I had a spotless character, enjoyed good credit, and possessed a thorough knowledge of my business; advantages which I easily persuaded myself would enable me to succeed without the actual possession of capital.— My business connections were scattered over various parts of the world, and generally ranked among the very best class of foreign merchants. I usually received orders by letter, sometimes I gave open credits to houses whose orders I could not otherwise secure,

B

but frequently I had remittances long before the merchandise could arrive at its destination. The trade was one of confidence, requiring both character and position for its development, and had I been prudent enough to confine myself strictly to this branch of the business, I would now, without doubt, have been a wealthy and successful merchant. At the end of my first year's operations my ledger showed a satisfactory balance to my credit. The year 1857 opened auspiciously, and I continued to prosper almost to the end of it, when a storm swept over the commercial world, which involved hundreds of firms in bankruptcy and ruin.

From the nature of my business it was scarcely possible I could escape, and although I succeeded in avoiding bad debts, I incurred indirect losses to a very considerable amount. In May, 1858, I paid a visit to the Continent, in order to ascertain on the spot how my connections there had weathered the recent storm. This visit resulted in a large increase of legitimate business, and up to this point I had taken no false step. Shortly afterwards, however, I was induced to embark in two different and distinct branches of trade, which led to my ruin. The first was the manufacture of novelties, which, after a large expenditure, I was obliged to relinquish, in consequence of my not having sufficient capital to make it profitable. The second was a mercantile business,

managed by an agent resident on the Continent.
This agent was without means, and, as I afterwards
found, without the abilities necessary for the position.
He had not long commenced operations when a
war broke out in Lombardy, which furnished his
customers with an excuse for rejecting the goods they
had ordered before prices began to recede. The consequence was that I had thousands of pounds' worth
of goods thrown upon my hands abroad, which resulted in large direct and still larger indirect losses.
It was at this juncture that I ought to have stopped
payment, but, being of a sanguine disposition, and
my regular business continuing to prosper, I hoped
the successes in the one branch would balance the
losses in the other, and I resolved to struggle on. I
paid a second visit to the Continent about this time,
which resulted in the formation of a partnership
with my agent, the business to be carried on in his
name. The new firm was debited with all the stock
on hand at cost prices, and in all future business the
profits were to be divided. I thought, by giving my
friend an interest in this branch of my business, that
I would lessen my losses on rejected stock and facili-
tate my escape from impending bankruptcy. I
arranged to draw bills on the firm at three months'
date, payable abroad, for such amounts as my partner
could see his way to meet at maturity. I also had a
private arrangement with my partner for obtaining

what I called accommodation bills. These were in the form of promissory notes, issued in my favour, and payable in London by myself; they were not to enter into the books of the firm, and I was to be entirely responsible for them. I may here also explain that the partnership between me and my agent was not known, except to the customers of the firm abroad and to my own clerks at home. Thus, under the pressure of large obligations I was not at the moment in a position to meet, joined to an extreme horror of the very idea of bankruptcy, involving as it did the loss of a lucrative and steadily-increasing branch of my regular business; I resorted to an expedient to preserve my character and position which I afterwards found the laws of my country declared to be a serious crime, to be expiated only by the complete and utter ruin of both.

During all this time my private and social relations were without reproach; neither was I without opportunity, gladly embraced, of doing good service to the trade with which I was connected, and also to my country. In the year 1860 I was chosen a director of the Chamber of Commerce in the city where my business was chiefly transacted. In connection with the international treaty between Great Britain and France, I was selected by my co-directors to classify and place average permanent values on the manufactures of the district, in order to regulate their admission under that treaty with France. I performed the task to the entire satisfaction of the Chamber, and was afterwards sent to Paris as one of a deputation appointed for the purpose of giving Mr. Cobden the most efficient aid towards the completion of his glorious, and happily successful, project. Owing to the very strong protectionist feeling on the part of the French manufacturers, great difficulties were encountered ; but, after the deputation had made two visits to Paris, they were finally overcome. It was universally acknowledged that if it had not been for the presence of practical men in Paris on that occasion, the treaty would have been completely inoperative, so far as concerned the important manufactures which I as one of the deputation represented. For my share in these transactions I received the thanks of the Lords of the Committee of Privy Council for Trade, also the commemorative medal from the French Government, with accompanying letter, * acknowledging my services, from M. Rouher, then Minister of Commerce and Agriculture at Paris.

During my second visit to Paris, in 1860, on public duty, I formed the resolution of breaking off my connection with the partner previously referred to, and of starting a business in Paris. I entered into negociations with a gentleman highly recommended to me with a view to partnership, and received from

* See Appendix.

my father the promise of cash to assist me in my new undertaking. Once fairly clear of the losing branch of my business I hoped very speedily to make up my previous losses, and the spring of 1861 was fixed upon for the opening of my Paris establishment. But my hopes were not destined to be realised. On looking into my affairs at the close of the year, I found, notwithstanding the satisfactory character and position of the legitimate branch of my business, and notwithstanding that my private expenditure did not amount to a tenth part of the profits on that branch, I had otherwise become almost hopelessly involved, and I accordingly resolved to stop payment. With this view, I disclosed to my principal creditor my position and intentions. Taking the manager of the firm into my confidence, I informed him of the assistance I expected to receive from my father, and the hopes I entertained of the results of my Paris business when once in operation. The consequence was that the firm offered to forego 1000*l.* of their claim against me, and to give me occasional assistance in cash to meet any other engagements if I would continue to carry on my business. At this time I owed them about 10,000*l.*, covered to a considerable extent by the accommodation bills I have already referred to; I must, however, explain that the character of these bills was known to the manager of the firm, and any banker or discounter could have readily satisfied himself as to their value by simply writing to the house in London where they were domiciled.

There were many considerations urging me to accept the offer now made to me. The present of 1000*l.*, the probable success of my Paris business, the approach of my money making season, joined to my horror of bankruptcy, all combined to induce me to alter my resolution to stop payment, and to inspire me with the hope that I would yet be able to retrieve my position and retain my good name. In a fatal hour I yielded to the temptation and closed with the proposals made to me, with the additional obligation that I was to pay off the 10,000*l.* due to the firm I have mentioned during the approaching season, and to give them good bills in exchange for the accommodation paper held by them. No sooner was this arrangement completed than I set about preparations for opening my Paris house. I refused to send any more goods to my old partner, and ordered him to wind up the business by the following May. I moreover resolved to having nothing more to do with accommodation bills, tore out all the leaves in my private letter book referring to these documents—a very fatal error, as I afterwards found —and exerted myself to pay off the claims of those of my creditors who knew my position. So well did I succeed, that by the end of April I had reduced

the 10,000*l*. claim to rather less than 5000*l*., or rather
to 4000*l*., taking into account the 1000*l*. conceded by
the firm previously mentioned. But before this I
had began to suspect that my friends did not mean
to adhere to the arrangement I had entered into
with them, one part of which was, that they were to
retire and return me the accommodation bills, on
getting good paper in their place. I had at this time
placed good bills in their hands to the extent of
3500*l*., but they refused to give up those they were
intended to replace until they arrived at maturity.

I began to fear that they would now compel me to
stop payment just when they supposed I should be
in possession of fresh funds for my Paris partnership,
and at a time when (with the bills in their possession,
which ought, according to agreement, to have been
in mine) they could rank on my estate for about
7000*l*., when with less than 4000*l*. I could have
settled the account. This, by the way, is what they
ultimately did, and had my estate yielded the respectable dividend they expected, instead of losing even
the 1000*l*. they promised to concede to me, they
would have been gainers to that amount by the
operation.

My transactions with this firm were in the position I have described when I started for the Continent with the view of opening my Paris business,
and of winding up my previous unlucky partnership.

This was the most successful journey I ever made. I visited Bremen, Hamburg, the interior of Germany, crossed through Switzerland to Lyons, where I appointed to meet my French traveller; visited with him all the large towns in France, and with my pocket-book full of valuable orders I found myself in London in less than four weeks from the time I left home. I arrived in London on a Wednesday, and telegraphed to the firm to which I have referred that I would call on them personally on the following Friday morning, to settle their claim and receive the bills they ought to have returned before.   *   *   *
On the Thursday evening, as I was preparing to leave the hotel for the railway station, I was suddenly and most unexpectedly arrested, and have not yet reached the spot I once loved to call my Home.

CHAPTER II.

MY FEELINGS ON FIRST ENTERING PRISON—TREATMENT AND EMPLOY-
MENT BEFORE TRIAL—MY TRIAL AND SENTENCE.

IT is impossible to give the faintest idea of my state of mind on finding myself a prisoner. The circumstances of my arrest, while in the midst of my arrangements for a long night journey to Scotland, flushed with success beyond my most sanguine anticipations, and impatient to accomplish my freedom from a burden which had long oppressed me, and which had latterly threatened to utterly bear me down, gave an overwhelming force and severity to the shock. Indeed, the sudden and undreamt of change in my destination, the sharp and complete extinction of all my hopes and plans, stunned me for the time, and I felt it must be a hideous dream. I refused to credit the evidence of my senses: the detective's touch, which still burnt upon my arm; the words of arrest, which still rang in my ears; his actual presence by my side—were but "false creations of the mind." I continued to think, as I walked along in that strange company, that I must still be on my way to the railway station; that I saw the glare of the lights, and mingled in the bustle of the platform, when the dark outline of a London lock-up met my bewildered eyes. We entered its grim and silent gates, the cell door was closed behind me, the lock was turned, and I and the reality were left alone. About that dark cheerless cell, its cold bare walls, its grated windows, its massive door, there was to me an awful certainty.

In an access of astonishment and grief I threw myself on the solitary bench, for they had not sought to mock my misery with the presence of a bed, and as thoughts of my wife and friends came upon me, I covered my face with my hands and wept. How long that flood of hot and bitter tears continued I know not, but they partially relieved my almost bursting head. I arose, and in the darkness paced my prison floor. Even in these terrible hours hope did not utterly forsake me. The swift revolution of Fortune's wheel had indeed left me crushed and mangled in its track, but I was not actually ground to powder. As I became more familiar with the reality of my situation, I began to take a calmer and more hopeful view of the future. As morning dawned, I had almost persuaded myself that I had only to see the manager of the firm who held the bills, for uttering which I had been arrested, and make certain explanations and proposals, to regain my liberty. With impatience, therefore, I awaited the hour, which I knew must come, when I would be removed from London to Scotland; and when, at last, the detective who was to accompany me opened my cell door, I almost welcomed him as a friend. We booked at Euston Square Station for the place which I intended to have gone to, under such widely different circumstances, the previous evening. My guardian performed his duty during this long and painful journey with kindness and consideration, and did not propose to put handcuffs upon me.

Arrived at our destination, I was marched through the police and sheriff's office to the common prison, and, to my utter astonishment and dismay, was prohibited for nine or ten days to have any communication with my friends. The single ray of hope which had sustained me on my weary journey, and illumined my darkest hour, was thus pitilessly excluded, and for the first time since my arrest I began to realise my true position. When I learnt that my arrest and incarceration in jail was noticed in all the newspapers, I felt that I was utterly and hopelessly ruined. No language could describe the anguish I endured as I thought of my wife and my friends, of the disgrace and humiliation which I had brought upon them, and of the separation, worse than death itself, which was in store for us. Yet, strange as it may appear, amid all the mental torture I then and

afterwards endured, I also experienced a certain
sense of relief in my mind from considerations which
would scarcely be expected to operate on one in my
situation. Those only who have been in difficulties
in business, who have borne the ceaseless strain on
body and mind which the burden of obligations, each
day rushing forward with ever increasing velocity for
liquidation, entails upon those who are honestly
striving to stem the ebbing tide of fortune, can fully
understand how relieved I felt at the thought that I
had no longer any bills to pay. Then a strong sense
of indignation towards my prosecutors mingled with
the wild and bitter current of my thoughts, and
prevented me from being overpowered and destroyed.
It was now but too clear to me that I was the victim
of a premeditated and heartless scheme, the successful issue of which was to protect my creditors from
loss indeed, but to involve me in utter ruin.

I saw, with feelings I cannot and dare not utter,
and which I now confess it was sinful in me to
cherish, that they had lured me on to the centre of
a great sea of ice ; that they had, when their opportunity came, broken it around me, and left me alone
and ΄helpless to struggle against inevitable doom.
Three of the six long weary months during which I
waited for trial were thus passed in a state of agony
bordering on the madness of despair. The hours
seemed magnified into days, and the weeks into

years ; and, as they dragged their slow length along, my mental anguish received a new and terrible ally. Although I was as yet in the eye of the law an innocent man, the miserable allowance of oatmeal which constituted my chief food, and which was in all respects inferior to the penal diet of the worst-behaved convict I ever met with in the English prisons, became loathsome to me, and the pangs of hunger were added to the mental torture I had till then alone endured. My cup of misery was surely filled to the brim !

With the recollection of what I suffered then, burnt, as it were, with a hot iron on my memory, I thank Almighty God that no fiend was ever permitted, even in my worst and weakest hour, to whisper suicide to my ear; but I now can understand how some have listened to the fell deceiver, and welcomed him, as friend and deliverer, to their arms. Fortunately for me, my early training and subsequent mode of life preserved me from any thought of this fatal solution to the problem of my life. I read my bible almost con-stantly, although my reading seemed only to add to the bitterness of my regrets and self-reproaches. These questions would constantly suggest themselves to me : "Could I ever have been a Christian ?" and "What will the enemies of Christianity think and say about my fall ?" Until one day about noon, as I was gazing through the window of my lonely cell, I saw, or

fancied I saw, a solitary star, and my thoughts were
gradually lifted from the cross of suffering to the
throne of Mercy, and (let philosophers and theolo-
gians explain it as they may) instantaneous peace of
mind followed the sight, or fancied sight, of that noon-
tide star! The load was removed which threatened
to crush my brain into lunacy, the "salt surf waves of
bitterness" were stilled, and within me there was peace.

The preparations for my approaching trial now
occupied the principal share of my attention. I had
already consulted a solicitor, and without telling him
the whole of my case, I learned from him that I could
not be tried at all if the Continental witnesses refused to come to Scotland. So advised, I began to
flatter myself with the belief that my case would
ultimately be abandoned for lack of evidence. I certainly wished that my late partner would come over
and testify to my partnership with him, which would
have cleared my name from dishonour so far as
related to the bills with which we were jointly concerned ; but, knowing there were other bills of a
similar character of which he knew nothing, I thought
it would be useless to attempt to clear myself on one
set of bills when I was unable to do so on them all,
and I consented to my friend being instructed by
my solicitor to remain at home. As, of course, it was
of the last importance to me that the witnesses in
connection with the other set of bills should also be

absent, my solicitor wrote to them to the same effect. I will here explain the reasons which induced me at this crisis to adopt a course which many of my readers, no doubt, will regard as an attempt to defeat the ends of justice. I did not for a moment desire to justify myself with regard to the bills in question. To utter bills of exchange for which no real value has been given is not justifiable, however common it may be, and to tender such bills in exchange for merchandise, and dishonour them at maturity, is flagrant dishonesty. Whatever may have been the amount of my guilt, of the intention to defraud any man I was as innocent as an unborn child. If I had had any such intention, the Bankruptcy Court would have been the safe and easy way to gratify it. Neither in these transactions did I ever suppose that I was offending the statute law of the country, since by the exercise of the same caution which enabled, and still enables, other men to tread very closely upon, but never to overstep, the limits of legality, I too might have kept myself secure from criminal prosecution. I considered myself justified, therefore, in availing myself of such means as were in my power to evade the operation of laws I had never consciously violated. But in all this I may have been, and probably was, in error ; I have no wish to extenuate or explain away any fault or crime of which I may have been guilty; I choose, rather, the language of penitence and confession ; and although I may never perhaps be forgiven by society, I shall cherish the hope of being more mercifully dealt with by Him who said, with reference to a greater sin than mine, "Go, and sin no more."

Thus the days and weeks passed away, while I still hoped and believed that no one would appear to witness against me. The prison diet now, however, began to tell seriously upon me.

In England and America I believe a prisoner is allowed to maintain himself, under certain restrictions, whilst he is waiting for trial; but in Scotland he is compelled to subsist on a diet which is considered the main ingredient in the punishment of the very lowest class of offenders whose sentences do not exceed a few months' imprisonment. The sense of punishment involved in this treatment—which would kill me now—was to some extent forgotten in the greater mental suffering I then endured, but the pangs of hunger and painful dreams about food frequently compelled me to think of my health. On making a complaint to the medical officer of the prison, he told me that as I was in good health he could only give me the choice of coffee and a slice of bread in lieu of the oatmeal breakfast; but on seeing the small quantity of bread I was to be allowed, compared with the bulk of the oatmeal porridge, I decided on not changing for the worse.

I did not wish to be treated differently from other prisoners, and therefore did not appeal to any higher authority. Indeed, I then imagined that as I was stronger and heartier than the majority of my miserable companions, I could subsist upon a meagre diet as well, if not better, than they. I now know from experience that I was wrong in this opinion, and that the man of strong digestion, accustomed to a generous diet, is likely to sustain more injury to his health by a sudden change to a very low scale of dietary, than those of weak digestion who have not been accustomed to any other. The only concession made to me was a slight addition to the time for exercise in the open-air cribs provided for that purpose. My legs, accustomed to much exertion, began to get stiff, and after I had been incarcerated for four or five months, one of my ankles occasionally pained me. The day fixed for my trial at last drew nigh, and so confident had I become that I should be liberated without a trial, that I had my clothes packed and ready to take abroad with me. I intended to leave the country for ever, and seek a new home in a distant land, where the prejudices of friends and society would not debar me from all the channels of honour and usefulness. I was removed a few days previous to the date fixed for my trial to the prison in the city where it was appointed to take place, and I then had my first experience of handcuffs.

At length the eventful morning arrived that I was led to believe would set me free. I entered the court with a beating heart, and was placed in the dock between two policemen. I felt ashamed to lift my head or to look around me, but I had seen as I entered that the space open to the public was crowded with the better class of citizens. The judges, of whom there were three, soon appeared and took their seats upon the bench, and began conversing with each other upon my indictment. One of them was over-heard saying, "It would be a very difficult case to prove." Meanwhile some consultation was taking place amongst the legal gentlemen in front of me, when my agent and counsel came and, for the first time, informed me that my trial might take place without the continental witnesses, and that sup-posing I was acquitted I could be tried again on two of the bills; that already there was a warrant out against me, and I should be arrested a second time on leaving the dock! The crown was willing, how-ever, they said, to accept a limited plea of guilt; that I would be sentenced to only a few months' imprison-ment, not longer perhaps than I would have to endure in suspense, waiting a second and perhaps a third trial, and that it would be better for me to tender the plea of guilt the crown was willing to accept!

This advice, so unexpected and so different from

what I had formerly received, given at the very last moment, had the effect of entirely unhinging my mind, and for the moment I seemed paralysed.

Of this I was conscious, however, that the continuance of suspense, that most painful of all suffering, combined with the compulsory oatmeal treatment of remanded Scottish prisoners, would kill me; still I could not bring myself to utter the words placed in my hands for that purpose; I waited, and hesitated, and wondered where the jury were, and why they were giving me so long to consider before going on with the business of the court. Time seemed to have been given me on purpose to confuse my mind, for the longer I pondered the more bewildered I became. At last, like a child who does almost mechanically as his parents bid it, I read from a paper these words: "I plead guilty to uttering two bills of exchange, knowing them to be fictitious." The judge in the centre asked the counsel for the crown if he accepted the plea, and on getting an answer in the affirmative, he whispered a second or two with his brother judge, whose son I believe prepared the case against me, and then pronounced sentence of penal servitude for a term of years that then seemed eternity to me I was removed from the court to the prison, stripped of my clothes, clad in the garb of the convict, and turned into a cell, there to writhe in tearless agony, and to indulge in bitter and unavailing regrets.

CHAPTER III.

THE paroxysm of grief and indignation which
followed my return to prison gradually subsided,
and after a few days I became in some measure resigned
to my fate, and determined as far as possible to make
the best of it. Indeed, in some respects the change
in my circumstances was for the better. The oatmeal
treatment, it is true, was still continued, but with
this difference that I now got more of it, and a still
further and most welcome addition of a pennyworth
of good milk and a pennyworth of eatable bread per
diem. I remained on this diet during the three
months and a-half which elapsed before I was removed
to England.* Unfortunately, during this time my
stomach, though craving for animal food, would not
accept the oatmeal, or chief portion of my diet, and

* Perth, where the diet is more liberal, was not then opened for
convicts.

accordingly I was in the practice of dividing it amongst my fellow prisoners.

I mentioned my case to the medical officer, but had to rest content with a little quinine and the assurance that I would be sent to England in a day or two, where I would get a few ounces of animal food daily. To add to my troubles, one of my ankles began to swell, but after some time, and by the application of flannel bandages, the swelling decreased and the limb seemed quite sound again.

These were not encouraging circumstances, however, under which to commence a long period of imprisonment, the less so, as from what I had observed, I feared that in the event of illness I should have to submit to a very limited amount of medical attendance. Probably, in consequence of being frequently imposed upon by the prisoners, and having private practice to attend to, doubtless of a more remunerative character, the medical officer was exceedingly rapid in his progress through the prison, and not more so in that than in his diagnosis and prescriptions. With the pangs of hunger constantly gnawing within me, and the dread of bad health and a ruined constitution haunting me day and night, I endeavoured by constant occupation to obtain some mitigation of my sufferings. I read all the books I could get hold of, wrote farewell letters to friends, hoping and believing that I would be sent to Western

Australia, as it was then the practice to do with all healthy convicts of my own age who had received similar sentences. I also seized every available opportunity of conversing with the old "lags," or convicts, about prison life, and it was here I received my first lessons in slang and thiefology, and began my study of the convict and his surroundings.

But I could not yet think of myself as a convict; I had the usual prejudice, or rather horror of the species, entertained by the middle class, and declined to accept the offer, made in kindness, of having a neighbour in the same cell with me. I was compelled, however, to take exercise for some minutes every day, together with another prisoner, and I was usually best pleased when I happened to be put into the same crib with one who had been a convict before. It was during these daily rounds that I witnessed with sadness the evil effects of sending boys or lads to prison for a few days or weeks for some petty theft, and placing them in constant contact and association with the habitual and reputed scoundrel and ruffian. These men are always willing to make a convert, and they generally succeed, for the battle is half won ere they bring their forces on the field. It is here that the juvenile offender is nursed in villainy, here he learns the inducements to crime, and from the lips of the hardened and experienced ruffian he hears of exploits and deeds of darkness, which inflame while they pollute his imagination, and he longs to be free that he might add some daring feat of wickedness to the catalogue he has heard. There can be no doubt that the indiscriminate association of all grades of criminals is one of the most prolific sources from whence our convict prisons receive their constant and foul supply. It was in one of these open-air cribs that I was initiated into the mysteries of prison politics and prison slang, for the convict has his "policy" as well as the government, and also his official, or rather professional nomenclature, in which he enshrouds its meaning. To be an adept in prison politics is, first of all to know and understand all the prison rules and regulations, not for purposes of obedience, but evasion ; to discern the disposition and habits of the prison officers, with the view of conciliating or coercing them into trifling privileges or concessions ; to know the various methods of treatment, diet, and discipline at the different prisons, and the character and disposition of their governors; to contrive to be sent to the prison which is supposed to be the most comfortable; and to know when and where good conduct and bad conduct will be productive of the best results in the way of removal or remission of sentence. In my solitude, and with the prospect before me of a long experience of such company, these conversations with my fellow-prisoners possessed a certain kind of interest for me. I was also always eager to learn as much as I could of their previous history, and the cause of their imprisonment. One day, as I was taking my daily outdoor exercise, I observed an old man in the convict dress cleaning the prison windows a short distance from me, and I asked my neighbour in the crib who he was. "O! that's a beauty," said he. "He was walking down the street lately, along with another chum like himself, when a gentleman noticed them and asked them into a photographer's to get their portraits taken, and gave them a shilling each as being the two ugliest specimens of the human race he had ever seen!"

"How long has he been in prison?" I enquired.

"Goodness knows!" he exclaimed; "I think about eight or nine-and-twenty years, and the longest sentence he ever had, except the first, was sixty days."

"What are his offences usually?"

"Oh, nothing but kicking up rows in the streets, or smashing a window. Last time it was for a fight with a poor man with a large family. He got up the fight on purpose, and as both were about to be apprehended, he says to the man he was fighting with, 'Jack, give me half-a-crown and I'll swear all the blame on myself;' poor Jack was glad to accept the offer, so when they were taken before the magistrate the old beauty said—'Please sir, it was me that assaulted that man, and as I am entirely in the fault I hope you will give me all the punishment.'

So Jack got out rejoicing, and the beauty got in, chuckling over his half-a-crown, and speculating on the feast he would get with it when his sixty days expired !"

"How long does he generally remain out of prison ?" I then enquired.

"Why" said my friend, "two days is a long time for him ; if he is beyond that time he will come to the prison and beg a meal !"

" Why does he not go to the poorhouse ?" I asked.

"Because he is more accustomed to the jail, and likes it better. He is generally employed in cleaning windows and other parts of the prison, and he likes a 'lark' with the prisoners, most of whom he knows !"

" Finding my companion so communicative I continued my enquiries, and asked him, " What young fellows are these in the next cell ?" "They have both been in the army," he replied. " One of them committed a small forgery, I think he forged the captain's order for some boots. He expected to get 'legged,'* and get out of the army, but he has been sucked in. They only gave him a few months' imprisonment, and he will have to go back to his regiment again when his time's up. His brother's now at Chatham, doing a four years 'legging,' but he hasn't to go back again to the army. This fellow swears he'll commit another crime as soon as he gets out !"

* Penal servitude.

Whether this threat of committing another crime was carried out or not I cannot tell, but in the earlier years of my imprisonment I came in contact with several prisoners who had committed offences for the purpose of getting out of the army. Of late years I have not met with any having been perpetrated with that motive.

Noticing a delicate, melancholy-looking young man opposite to us, I enquired who he was. "O! I pity that man very much," said my friend. "He has got a sentence of twenty-one years' penal servitude, and is as innocent of the crime as the child unborn."

"How do you know he is innocent?" I asked, in amazement.

"The guilty man has turned up, now that they cannot punish him, and confessed."

Shortly after this conversation took place, I had an opportunity of learning, from the lips of one of the principal offenders in the case for which this young man was unjustly punished, the following particulars in reference to it, which I give in my informant's own words:—"I and other two miners like myself went to a horse-race a few weeks ago. Towards evening we got a little on the spree, and I asked my two chums to come along and see a woman of my acquaintance. This woman was kept by a gentleman in the neighbourhood, but this was only known to a few. She was about forty years of age, and although

she was supposed by some to be 'fast,' I knew long
before that she was 'loose.' Well; as we were all
enjoying ourselves in this woman's house, who should
come in but her brother ! and so, to clear her character
with him, she swore a rape against us. But the
worst of it was, that that poor married man there
got convicted instead of one of us. When we ran
from the house, the other fellow split out from us,
and after we got away a bit, we met the married
man. As we were chatting together we were all
three arrested. The woman, it seems, had an
ill-will either to that man or his wife, and she swore
against him on that account. And we have all
three got twenty-one years a-piece."

I was glad to hear afterwards that this man got
his liberty after suffering six months' imprisonment.
But had it not been for great exertions on the part
of his friends, he would have had to pay the full
penalty. I have known, in the course of my prison
experience, about a dozen well authenticated cases of
innocent convictions, but only two of them succeeded
in getting a pardon. The one after enduring about
eighteen months' imprisonment, the other a shorter
period, but strange to say his pardon arrived on the
very day of his death in prison.

I have generally observed in cases of rape, and
crimes of that kind, when the female was advanced
in life, that the crimes were not so black in reality

as they were represented in the newspapers, and that the offenders, if not made actually worse in prison, would be much more easily cured than the thief genus, who require special, and as I think, very different treatment to that which they now receive.

In this prison I also made the acquaintance of a professional "cracksman," or burglar. He was a man of fair education, good appearance, and considerable natural ability; much above the average of his professional brethren. He had been living luxuriously in London, on the fruits of his professional industry and skill. Till now he had escaped all punishment, with the exception of a few months' imprisonment, for a "mistake" committed at the outset of his professional career. In answer to my enquiries as to his case, he volunteered the following information :—

"A few weeks ago, one of my 'pals' (companions) showed me the advertisement of a Scottish jeweller, wherein he boasted of his safe having successfully resisted the recent efforts of a gang of burglars. I said to my pal, 'Get Bob, and let us go down to-morrow by the mail train to Scotland, and we will see what this man's safe is like.' We all three came down here a few weeks ago, inspected the jeweller's premises, and decided on doing the job through an ironmonger's shop at the back. We had got the contents of the ironmonger's till, and were just through

the intervening back wall, when the 'copper'*
heard us, and signalled for another 'bobby'* to
come and help him.   Out I sprang, and had a fight
with the policeman, and got knocked down insensible.
My pal bolted and got off; Bob and I got 'copt,'† and
as we had first-class tools on us, new to the authorities
here, they have given it us rather hot."

"Do you think you could have opened the safe?
I understand those patent locks are very difficult to
pick," I remarked.

"Oh!" said he, "I would not waste time trying to
pick the lock.   Drill a hole and get in the 'jack,'
and I can bring power to bear on it sufficient to open
any safe.   The great thing is to be able to get the
time, the work I can easily do; then Bob, my pal, is
one of the best blacksmiths in England, and as true
as steel.   I always take him with me in a job of that
sort."

It so happened that I had a very good opportunity
of proving that the burglar's high opinion of his
"pal's" ability was not without foundation.   On our
removal to England, the "cracksman," was leg-ironed
to me as an additional security against his making
his escape.   There were five couples besides ours, and
after we arrived at our destination, and whilst the
prison blacksmith was engaged hammering and punch-
ing off my irons, Bob, with a smile of contempt at

* Policeman.   † Caught.

his efforts, took up some tools that lay beside him and liberated the other five couples before the blacksmith had freed me and my clever companion.

The chief incident which occurred during my imprisonment in Scotland, was a conspiracy among the convicts to murder the night officer and make their escape in a body. I was not considered "safe" for the job, and knew nothing of it until it had miscarried. The chief conspirator was my friend the "cracksman," who made tools out of portions of his bedstead, that opened not only the lock of our own cell, but that of every other cell in the prison, if required. The prisoners were generally in couples in each cell at that time, and the plan agreed upon was as follows : One of the convicts was an old man subject to fits, and it was arranged that he was to feign a fit for the occasion ; the assistance of the night officer was to be called, who was to have his "light put out" by the fellow prisoner of the one in fits, who was a strong muscular fellow. Meanwhile the "cracksman," whose cell was opposite, was to unlock the cell doors of all the prisoners in the plot. This dark and desperate scheme was frustrated, however, by a little lad, who had heard two of the convicts conversing about it. His term of imprisonment expired on the day preceding the night fixed for the accomplishment ; and he gave information to the governor, who placed officers with fire-arms in

the ward all night. Next morning the suspected
prisoners were searched, and the lock-picking instruments were found on the "cracksman," and there the
affair ended. The only result which followed the
discovery of the plot, so far as I could discover, was
that we were removed from this prison to England
rather earlier than we otherwise should have been.

Previous to our removal, the governor, who was a
very sensible man compared with those under whom
I was afterwards placed, told me that I was about to
be sent to England along with some of the worst
characters he had ever known; that they were all
leaving the prison with the character of conspirators,
except myself; that he had given me the best character he could give to any prisoner, and that he hoped
and believed I would reap the benefits attaching to good
conduct, and be liberated long before my companions.
But I was not born under a fortunate star. Almost
all my companions had longer sentences than I had.
Bob and the cracksman had two years longer; but as
they managed to secure the convict's prize, they were
sent out to Australia, and were liberated, I believe,
two years before me. Some prisoners with sentences
twice as long as mine were also liberated earlier than
I was; and I remember alluding to this circumstance in a letter to my friends, written when I had
been about four years and a-half in prison; and for
doing so my letter was suppressed.

The night of my departure for England at last arrived, and I found myself for the first time placed in heavy leg-irons, along with eleven others. We were put into the prison-van for the railway station; and as soon as we were seated in the carriage there commenced a scene which baffles all description. Some of my fellow-prisoners commenced shouting, some screamed and laughed, others mocked and jeered, whilst above all curses loud and deep hurtled through the stifling air, and made night hideous with the sound. Their yells and oaths still ring in my ears, and that which was to my companions a scene of the utmost jollity and mirth was to me the nearest approach to hell my imagination had ever conceived. It was a cold spring night that witnessed my degrading departure; when I arrived at my destination in Yorkshire one of my legs was considerably swollen. It is a cold spring night now; that swollen limb has for years been in the tomb, and the dismembered trunk, on its "Ticket of Leave," has not yet returned to its long-lost home.

D

CHAPTER IV.

ON my arrival at the Yorkshire prison I and
my companions were subjected to a new, and
to me most painful operation. I am quite well
aware that it would be next to useless, if not quite
hypocritical, in one in my position to lay claim to
any considerable delicacy of feeling, or to appear to
be over scrupulous in matters of common decency.
But there will occasionally, however, be found even
amongst convicts those who will bear a pretty long
period of imprisonment, during which they are subjected to a variety of contaminating influences, and
yet not have their moral sensibilities completely
destroyed. Of these I was one, and I felt that the
treatment which I had now to undergo was conceived in a barbarous spirit, and was well fitted to
destroy utterly any feelings of self-respect which my
previous experiences had still left me. Every part

of my body was minutely inspected immediately on my arrival, in order that I might not take any money or tobacco into the prison.

Doubtless it is very desirable, and even necessary, that every precaution should be taken to prevent such articles finding their way into prisons—at least on the persons of prisoners—but the fact remains that, notwithstanding these inspections, both money and tobacco do find their way into prison, and are every day in common use amongst the prisoners. Prisoners will have tobacco, and tobacco cannot be got without money, so that both must be obtained; and the result has been that the more rigorous the inspection, the greater the ingenuity required to evade it. The trials of skill and invention which goes on between the convict and the inspector, like those between artillery and iron plates, have as yet only proved that, given the power of resistance, the power of overcoming it will be found. One of my fellow-prisoners verified the truth of this conclusion by taking five sovereigns into prison with him, notwithstanding all the care and experience exercised by the inspector.

I now got the first taste of animal food I had had for about ten months. So keen was my appetite that I could have relished any cooked carrion even, if it had come in my way. I also got potatoes, the very skins of which I devoured with great gusto. It was very curious that at this time

I preferred salt to sugar, or anything that was sweet, and I used to suck little lumps of salt for the first few days I had the opportunity of doing so with as much relish as children do their sugar plums. The bread at this prison was excellent, and the food generally of good quality.

The day after my arrival I was ordered to strip a second time for the medical inspection, and as a considerable time elapsed before my turn came, I had to remain standing in that state with my swollen leg rather longer than was good for me. When the inspection was concluded my leg was ordered to be bandaged, and some medicine was given to me daily. I now had my hair cut in the approved prison fashion, and was put into a cell to sew mats, in a standing posture. In this employment, relieved by a short period of daily out-of-door exercise, I passed one of the three and a-half months I was in this prison. The two chaplains before whom I was taken shortly after my arrival, were extremely kind to me during the whole time I remained. One of them had done much good among the prisoners, and had been of great service to many of them by getting them employment after they were liberated; thus removing the greatest obstacle in the way of a permanent reformation of the prisoner.

I recollect the first Sunday I spent in this prison. I was very nearly getting reported to the governor for a very unintentional violation of the prison rules. In accordance with these rules, convicts were not allowed to turn their heads in any direction in chapel, and if they did so they were taken by the attendant officer before the governor, who punished them for disobedience. I cannot but suppose that those who framed these rules had some good end in view, in being so stringent in the matter of posture in the religious services. The difficulty with me was to discover whether the spiritual welfare of the prisoners, or the preservation of a more than military discipline amongst them, even in matters of religion, had appeared to them to be of the greater importance.

It is probable, however, that neither of these considerations decided the question, but that the principal object of these regulations was to preserve in the convict mind, even in the act of worship, the idea of punishment in a perfectly lively and healthy condition. Be that as it may, on my first Sunday in chapel, with my English prayer-book before me, which was then quite new to me, I found myself quite unable to follow the chaplain in the services in which he was engaged, and to which I was also a perfect stranger. Turning over the leaves of the prayer-book, in the vain attempt to find out the proper place, and happening to cast my eyes over the shoulder of the prisoner in front of me in order to find it, the movement caught the eye of the officer,

who sat watching every face, and I saw from his
stare, and the frown which gathered under it, that
I had committed a grave offence. Immediately I
resumed my proper attitude and sat out the service
as rigid as my neighbours, and so escaped the
threatened punishment. Only on one other occasion
did I transgress the prison rules : while at work I felt
the pain in my leg become almost insupportable, and
in order to relieve it I took rest, although still continuing to sew. For doing so I received a short
reprimand. The state of my leg now became a cause
of great anxiety to me, and rendered my out-door
exercise a source of pain, instead of a means of
relief from the monotony of my prison occupation.
This exercise was taken in a circle, keeping a certain
number of yards distant from another prisoner, and
we were forbidden to speak or even to look round.
Once or twice during the period of exercise we had
to run instead of walk. The running I found very
painful and injurious to my leg, and I petitioned the
doctor to be excused from it, but was refused. There
was nothing for it but to hop along, every step giving
me great pain. Until one day I made a false step,
the consequences of which compelled me to give up
walking altogether. My knee became inflamed, and
I was ordered to lie in my hammock in my cell.
Some pills were prescribed for me, which I soon found,
from the state of my gums, contained mercury. As I

knew that the cause of my complaint was the want of proper nourishment, I fancied the doctor had mistaken my case when he prescribed for me, and I ventured to speak to him about it. He did not appear pleased at my making any allusion to medicine. The pills were discontinued, but I was put on a change of diet for a month, which consisted in taking away my meat, soup, and potatoes, and giving me instead a dish of what was by courtesy termed "arrow-root," but which the prisoners more accurately designated "cobbler's paste." Under this regimen it will readily be believed my condition every day became worse, and at last, after being nearly two months confined to my cell, I got the order of removal to the hospital.

I remember—oh ! how well ! with what pain I crawled to it on all fours, and slid down stairs on my back without any assistance. In this way I managed to reach the sick-room, and the first object that attracted my attention on entering, was a convict at the point of death. A stream of blood was rushing from his mouth, which choked him just as I was placed in the next bed. Another convict, a Scotch shepherd, had died only a few days previously, from the effects of the treatment he received in the Scotch prisons previous to his trial. I may here mention that I met with several instances of deaths occurring in English prisons in consequence of the treatment the prisoners had received before trial in Scotland.

In the majority of these cases the period of detention before trial was six or seven months. I also heard of one case, which did not come within my own observation, however, where the prisoner who died was innocent of the crime with which he was charged, and that his widow intended to prosecute the authorities for damages. Whether she did so or not I never learned.

For about a month I lay in this hospital, but no improvement could be reported in the state of my health. In addition to the physical pain I endured, I was a prey to the most acute mental agony. I could feel that my originally strong constitution was being gradually undermined, and that the poison of disease which would never be eradicated from my system was, through ignorance or negligence, slowly and surely increasing within me. And then the possibility of losing my limb altogether was a thought which now and again forced itself upon me and made the warm blood curdle in my veins. All this time I knew, and the knowledge gave additional poignancy to my sufferings, that with care and proper surgical treatment I could easily have been cured ; but I dared not open my mouth in the way of suggestion or complaint, I had already been taught, by bitter experience, the folly of that. Through all the hours of my imprisonment I had learnt to look forward through the darkness of my nearer future to the day of my liberation as to a bright unsetting star. Its clear white ray pierced the clouds which hung dark and heavy over me, and shed light and hope within me, for it told me that behind these clouds there was a light, and a day which would yet dawn upon me, wherein I could work and redeem the past! But now the strong bright spirit of hope appeared to have forsaken me. As I lay upon my bed and gazed out of the window, watching the birds dart hither and thither in a clear blue sky, thoughts of the time when I should be free as they arose in my mind, but failed to cheer my desponding heart. Through the silent hours of night I have watched, from my bed of pain, the myriad stars shining in the midnight sky, glancing glory from far-off worlds, but I sought in vain among that radiant silent throng for mine. And I would think of the day when diseased and a cripple I should be cast out into the world alone, with the brand of the convict, like the mark of Cain, upon my brow, without friends, without sympathy, without hope, useless, purposeless, to eat the bread of charity, and die a beggar in the streets, with only these cold bright eyes above to witness at the last. Can it be wondered at, if under the influence of these feelings I began to repine against that Providence which had so roughly shaped my life, and to think with bitterness of the imperfection of all merely human justice ? I had met with men whose whole life had been spent in con-

stant warfare against society, and who had no other
intention on regaining their liberty than to continue
the struggle to the bitter end—the murderer; cheer-
ful and complacent over the verdict of manslaughter;
the professional garotter, in whose estimation human
life is of no value, troubled only at being so foolish
as to be caught; the polished thief and the skilled
housebreaker, every one of them sound in wind and
limb, intent only on their schemes and "dodges" to
extract the sting from their punishment, or in planning
new and more heinous crimes, and all longing for
the time when they and society could cry "quits,"
and they be at liberty to pursue their career of
villainy. With these, the vilest of the vile, and also
with the hoary criminal who knew no home save the
prison, who preferred it to the poorhouse, and to
whom its comforts were luxuries and its privations
but trifles of no account, I was condemned to mingle.
Repentant for what I had done in the past, capable
and resolved to make amends in the future, having
already suffered for my crime loss of friends,
character, everything almost that is dear to man,
I was also condemned to lose my health, my limb,
to be deprived of my only means of future subsist-
ence, and to endure more years of degradation and
suffering in prison than many of my wretched companions, who had committed heinous crimes and to
whom penal servitude was no punishment!

Such were some of the bitter reflections upon our criminal laws and prison regulations in which, under the pressure of severe mental and bodily suffering, I then indulged. Writing now, in a calmer and less indignant mood, I still commend them, and my subsequent experiences to the consideration of thoughtful men, and I leave it with them to decide whether the system maintained in our "model prisons," of putting all prisoners, whatever their character and antecedents, who have similar sentences, on a footing of perfect equality, and in constant association with each other, is fitted to serve the purposes of even human justice; and whether it is not more likely to promote than to prevent the growth of crime.

I had now been about a month in the hospital when the order came for my removal to a regular Government Convict Establishment, in Surrey. I was in a very unfit state for such a journey; I could not walk a single yard, even with assistance. My knee was so swollen that no trouser would go over it, but yet the journey had to be made, and on my arrival in Surrey I had to be carried by two prisoners to the hospital.

CHAPTER V.

THE Surrey prison in which I was doomed to spend nearly five years of my life is a somewhat spacious looking building, situated in a healthy locality, and fitted up for the accommodation of about 660 prisoners. It is built in the shape of the letter E. The centre abutments are occupied as a chapel and work-room; the end wings are divided into cells, with an underground flat fitted up as a school and a Roman Catholic chapel. The upper story of the main portion of the building is divided into cells, which are the best specimens of the human cage yet constructed. The under flat is divided into eighteen rooms of various dimensions, some containing seven, others eight and twelve, and the largest twenty-four beds. The middle flat is in constant use as an hospital, and is divided into four wards, containing accommodation for 150 patients. Very frequently, however, while I was here that number was exceeded, and other portions of the prison were often appropriated to hospital use.

As I was for upwards of two years after my arrival an inmate of one of these hospital wards, I may here give an outline of the routine of our daily life there.

At half-past five every morning the great bell rang, and the nurses and convalescent patients started out of bed, washed and dressed, made their beds, rubbed their metal chamber-service as bright as silver—a remarkable contrast in that respect to the metal dinner dishes—dusted and cleaned the ward, which was usually kept remarkably tidy and clean. About half-past six breakfast was on the table. This meal consisted of very weak tea and dry bread for the majority, with an egg, or half-an-ounce of butter for the few who were supposed to be dangerously ill or dying. In the interval between the breakfast time and nine o'clock the patients' wounds were dressed by the nurses, and medicines served out by the officers of the ward; those patients not immediately under treatment having liberty to read or chat with each other. Before I left, however, the attempt was being made to prohibit this reading and talking, and to combine more punishment with the cure of disease.

The two medical officers generally began their rounds of examination about nine o'clock. As they

entered the room "Attention !" was called, when all
the prisoners out of bed stood up, and as the doctors
passed, noting down on a ticket the date and remarks
on each man's complaint, they were saluted by the
patients in the military fashion.   The doctors' visit
over, the patients were assembled for prayers; after
which, and until the dinner-hour — a quarter to
twelve—the time was spent in out-door exercise.
From twelve till two the patients sat on their stools
reading or gossiping.   At two they went out again
to exercise.   At half-past three they were again assembled for prayers.   About five they got tea and
dry bread, as at breakfast; and at eight o'clock they
were all in bed.

The dinner of the patients varied according to the
nature of their disease.   The majority were served
with the regular hospital dinner, which consisted of
soup, potatoes, and what the dictary boards called
"Ten ounces of mutton."   With respect to the latter
item, however, I fancy there must have been some
mistake, although I have heard the prisoners charac-
terize it in different and much stronger terms.
Whether there be any mistake or not, *five* ounces,
or it might occasionally be six ounces with the bone,
is all the prisoners receive, and if complaint was
made the invariable answer was, that it "Lost four
ounces in the cooking."   I am not sufficiently skilled
in the culinary art to be able to say whether or

not ten ounces of mutton loses four ounces in cooking, but the great majority of prisoners did not believe it; and the evil effects of placing ten ounces on a board for the public to see, and five or six ounces in the dish for the prisoner to eat, are very great.

The old maxim, "Set a thief to catch a thief," was based on a shrewd acquaintance with human nature, and convicts are usually very quick in discovering discrepancies of the kind to which I have alluded; and it is not to be wondered at if they put the very worst construction upon them. In any case, if it forms any part of our prison discipline to inculcate moral principles, or to instil into the convict mind a regard for truth and honesty, it is surely of the utmost importance, indeed absolutely necessary, that the prison authorities, their only instructors, should be beyond suspicion. As entertaining books and newspapers are not allowed him, the convict has nothing else to talk about but the conduct of his jailers, and foolish prison gossip; and any subject of the kind I have mentioned is eagerly discussed with very injurious results to all concerned.

To return to my own case : after being carried upstairs to the hospital, I was inspected by the medical officer, and ordered into one of the largest wards, containing thirty-six beds, on one of which I was

destined to pass many long and painful months. On
the following morning my knee was examined by
both the prison surgeons. Unfortunately they seemed
to differ in opinion as to the treatment it should receive. The senior officer, who took charge of my
case, wished to make a stiff joint, whilst his junior
thought it should be lanced and poulticed, to take
out the matter, which by this time was creating an
abscess in the joint. Had I been allowed to express
my opinion on the subject I would have supported
the latter mode of treatment; but a convict dare
not utter a word with respect to medical treatment.
I was accordingly obliged to lie in one position
for three months with my leg strapped to a long slab,
and to use a lotion which proved very injurious
to it. During these three months I suffered the
most intense pain. I not only could not get out of
bed, but I could not change my position in it; and,
to add to the wretchedness of my situation, I could
not read; and finally I could not even sleep. My
food, however, was better and more abundant than
it had been hitherto. At first I was allowed a little
porter and some very inferior beef-tea, in addition to
the ordinary second-class hospital diet.

Some time after, when my knee was being frequently leeched, I said to the doctor that, if he
thought it necessary to take more blood from me
I would feel very grateful for a mutton chop in lieu

of the beef-tea. This he at the time very snappishly refused, but next morning he appeared to have seen the reasonableness of my request, and allowed me the chop. Being always truly grateful when I obtained any concession of this kind, and always civil and polite to those with whom I was brought into contact, whether officers or prisoners, I received more favourable consideration than the generality of my neighbours; and I had nothing to complain of, so far as regarded diet, during my subsequent stay in the hospital.

After a few weeks of great suffering to me, it became quite evident that my leg was not to get better under the treatment prescribed for it, but was rapidly getting worse. The knee was now so sensitive that the tread of any person's foot passing near the bed caused me excessive pain. I was afraid to sneeze for the same reason, and at last so excruciating did the pain become that I begged and prayed to have my leg cut off. The idea of losing it, so horrible to me a few months previous, was altogether overpowered by the frightful torture, which night and day it now entailed upon me. I was again inspected about this time by a stranger doctor, and immediately after he left, my leg was lanced and poulticed. But the remedy came too late, for the time had come when I must either sacrifice my life, or give life a chance by the sacrifice of my leg. My readers can imagine for themselves what

E

it must be to have the flesh cut, and the bone sawn through at the thickest part of the thigh. I fear I cannot give a more lucid description of the surgical operation. I was put under the influence of chloroform, which had to be administered a second time before the surgeons had completed their work, and with the exception of a momentary pang in the interval between the doses, I felt no pain whatever. The operation was skilfully performed, and occupied altogether about half-an-hour.

I was removed from the large ward, and placed in a small room by myself, with a prisoner to wait upon me, and for three or four days after the operation my life was despaired of by the medical officers. Strangely enough I did not feel so hopeless about my case. I felt a whispering within that seemed to tell me I should not die then. With the exception of the pain caused by the first few dressings of the wound, and a sharp violent twinge that seized the stump on my going to sleep, causing it to start some inches from the pillow on which it rested, I did not now experience anything to compare with my previous sufferings. The head surgeon also relaxed from his customary silent, stingy, and cold hearted manner, and became generous, and even kind to me. I had been in the habit of writing to my friends that I felt comfortable enough under the circumstances, in order to keep up their spirits about me, but now I could and

did express genuine feelings of gratitude, and until I
wrote a letter to the late Mr. Cobden, more than a
year afterwards, I believe I remained a favourite with
the chiefs of the establishment. I had now become
a cripple for life, and as I reflected upon all that these
words involved in relation to my future history, and
the circumstances which had entailed upon me a loss
so irretrievable, I thought, amongst other things
how easily, and still how fatally a little carelessness,
negligence, or ill-temper on the part of our convict
surgeons, may influence the future life and conduct
of their convict patients. They are, without doubt,
subjected to many vexations, and much annoyance,
and their temper receives daily provocations. They
have to deal professionally with a class of men who,
as a rule, cannot be believed or trusted; who are as
likely as not to give a false description of their complaint, and in many instances to do all in their power
to frustrate the efforts made to relieve it. They have
to discover not only what the disease is in real
patients, but also frequently to detect well planned
and well sustained imposture in those who are not
diseased at all. The latter is a much more difficult
task in many cases than the former, as I will subsequently show, and it has a tendency to sour the
temper and harden the heart, which the former does
not. I do not imagine that the medical men in our
convict establishments are naturally less warm-hearted,

less nobly devoted to their profession than their brethren outside, but it will not be disputed that the peculiar nature of their practice has a tendency to make them so. Were one hundred doctors each to have a patient for whom they had daily, for weeks, and even for months, been doing all that humanity and professional skill could suggest in order to relieve him, let us suppose of great suffering, and one fine morning to see the patient leap out of bed, laugh, and snap his fingers in their faces, and tell them that there had been nothing the matter with him all the while!—ninety-nine of them would probably look upon the next patient with some suspicion, and if deception was at all frequent, the really diseased would come in time to suffer even at the hands of the most tender and humane amongst them. I blame these "schemers" and "impostors" therefore for much of the apparent sourness, indifference to, and sometimes cruel neglect, if not positive aggravation of suffering, which I have noticed in the manner and treatment of most of the convict surgeons I have met with. I have seen the imperative necessity that exists for periodical inspection of our convict hospitals by competent medical men, not otherwise connected with them, in order to protect the "innocent patients," if I may use the term, from the indifference, mismanagement, and even punishment they are often compelled to undergo, because of the prejudices contracted by the prison officials, the result of a long experience perhaps of imposture and deception. Under the present system the resident medical superintendent has the lives of his patients at his sole disposal, and it is a very dangerous thing for a convict patient to offend the medical officers in any way, and of course the more so if they happen to be of a cruel or vindictive disposition. My own case was in some respects an instance of this. The experience I gained in the Yorkshire prison, after I had ventured to insinuate to the doctor there that he had not quite understood the nature of my complaint, kept my mouth hermetically closed during the ill-concealed disagreement between the two doctors here as to the method of my cure. The chief medical officer at this prison was very much disliked by the majority of the patients, particularly by the young prisoners in the early stages of consumption. The cause of this, was supposed to be the desire to keep the hospital well filled with patients, and to have the greater proportion of them of the class who were content to be idle without craving for " extras." He could thus keep the cost per head lower than the medical officers at other prisons, and obtain the greater credit at head-quarters. Young consumptive patients he found to be too expensive, and they were accordingly made uncomfortable. His junior, on the other hand, although blunt in his manner and speech, was held in general esteem. He seemed to have his heart in the profession, and endeavoured to cure complaints deemed curable without reference to the expense of the diet, if it contributed to the end he had in view.

In another chapter I shall again allude to this subject, and give a number of cases which came within the range of my own observation, to prove the justice of some of the reflections I have made on the want of periodical inspection of our prison hospitals. In the meantime my stump continued to discharge matter. An abscess formed and retarded the healing of the wounds and it was not till I discovered a cure myself that it showed any symptoms of healing. The cure was to hold the stump under a tap of cold water, using friction afterwards. This I continued to do long after the wound had finally closed.

CHAPTER IV.

ABOUT two months after the amputation of my leg, feeling and believing that my health would never be restored in confinement I wrote a petition to the Home Secretary, in the expectation that I would be as mercifully considered as my predecessors in misfortune. While my petition was under consideration I was encouraged in my expectations by the fact that one of my companions who had nothing the matter with him but a dislocated hip joint, was liberated on medical grounds three or four years before his time was up. My hopes were somewhat damped, however, by another circumstance which just then occurred. The prison director arrived on his monthly visit, and on passing through the ward, the medical officer who accompanied him stopped at the foot of my bed and informed him that I was the man whose leg he had amputated, and that I was "quite well now!" The director, seeing me in bed and looking very poorly, and noticing the general stare with which the doctor's remark was received, asked in a somewhat doubtful way, "Is he quite well?" "Oh! yes quite well," the doctor replied; and off they went.

I was sixteen months in hospital after the above remark was made, and I was then unable to get up to have my bed made, nor did I leave my bed during the whole winter and spring that succeeded! I received an answer to my petition, shortly after the visit to which I have referred, in the usual form of an official negative, "Not sufficient grounds." Being now free from acute pain, I conversed freely with my companions, and taught some of them to spell, read, and cypher. After I was able to get out of bed I read aloud for an hour every evening, for the benefit of all the patients. In time I became popular, and intimate with many of them. I wrote letters and petitions for them, encouraged them with good advice, and succeeded in obtaining considerable influence over them.

In return for these trifling services, which also to some extent relieved the monotony of the long period I spent in hospital, they told me their history and experiences. I learnt their slang and thiefology, and as a theorist became tolerably conversant with all the mysteries by which the professional thief and scoundrel preys upon society.

The first of my companions who attracted my

attention was a young Scotchman. He appeared to be a very strong hearty fellow, but when he attempted to walk, he was the most pitiable looking cripple imaginable, and excited the sympathy of all who saw him. His sentence was twenty-one years, four of which he had undergone at this time. He had been invalided home from the convict establishment at Bermuda, was shipwrecked off the Isle of Wight on the return voyage, and had been some months in the hospital previous to my arrival. He was in the habit of being carried up and down stairs to exercise on the backs of the nurses, and was getting full diet and porter. About four months after my arrival, he one morning suddenly started out of bed, shouted " Attention," at the top of his voice, in defiance of the prison rules, and ran about the room like a lamplighter, to the utter amazement of all present. This man was what the prisoners term a "schemer," and he was certainly the very best actor of his class I ever met with. It will be acknowledged that he played his part well, when even during the shipwreck he had never made the slightest attempt to move, and kept up the deception for many months in a prison hospital, where the majority of the patients are put down as " schemers" unless they have an outward sore, or some natural malady with ‹ palpable external symptoms. When the doctor came his rounds, he could do nothing but

stare at the fellow, who started up and told him with
a laughing countenance that he had had a dream in
the night, about being miraculously cured, and in the
morning he found he could walk as well as ever he
did.   The doctor never opened his lips; the patient
was discharged, and although the other patients cried
aloud that he ought to be punished, no further notice
was taken of the matter.

This "schemer," I learned, had been a great suf-
ferer from pleurisy at Bermuda, and was very weak
when he was put on board ship, where he commenced
his scheme; and had it not been for new regulations
which were then put in force, there is no doubt he would
have accomplished his object, which was "Liberation
on medical grounds."   He had petitioned the Home
Secretary shortly before he threw his crutches aside,
declaring that he had met with an accident at Bermuda from a stone falling on his back, and so injur-
ing the spine that both his legs were paralysed.
He had received a reply to the effect that his petition would be answered so soon as the authorities
heard from Bermuda the particulars of the accident,
and it was a few days after this that the miraculous
visitation took place.

I asked him why he did not wait for the final
answer to his petition before exposing his scheme?
" Oh," he replied, " I knew very well if they wrote to
Bermuda I should get no time off.   I met with no

accident, although I said so in my petition." " You
will be very fortunate," I said, " if you get the customary remission after this affair, I fear they will
punish you ? " Look here," said he, " I have another
scheme in my head, and you will see I'll not fail this
time. I'll get out to Australia, and by the time I
arrive I will be due for my liberty. " Well, that will
certainly be better for you than being kept eight or
nine years longer in prison here; but how are you to
manage to get abroad unless the authorities choose to
send you ?" " Oh ! I will work that. I'll now be as bad
in my conduct as possible; and I'll half murder
some of the officers if they don't send me away; and
that very soon too."

True to his threat, the fellow commenced a course
of bad conduct, knowing it would ensure his passage to Western Australia ; and in a comparatively
short time he gained his object, and I have no doubt
he is now at liberty abroad.

About the time the above conversation took place
another " schemer " arrived, and was located a few
beds from me. He had been a clerk in a government office, was respectably connected, and a very
intelligent young man. He pretended he could not
use his legs. The doctor's eye being now somewhat
opened, he told him there was nothing the matter
with him, recommended him to get well again as
fast as possible, and threatened him with the electric

battery, and even hot irons, if that did not succeed.. The prisoner did not take advice, however, and the battery was tried upon him. After being stripped several times, and made to cry out with pain, to the great amusement of his fellow-prisoners, he ultimately took to crutches; first two, then one, with a stick ;. then the stick only; then nothing at all. He was afterwards removed to another prison.

I saw several other cases, similar to the one I have just mentioned, of pretended loss of the use of the legs, or partial inability to walk; but as there was no marked difference in the cases, I need not notice them. There was, however, an amusing incident connected with one of them which I may mention. This prisoner was allowed a little porter every day, which was served out about one o'clock. One day at that hour he happened to be in an adjoining room with his crutches (he could walk a little) when another prisoner cried out, "Porter, porter; quick,. quick?" On hearing this cry, and afraid of losing his liquor, he bolted out, ran down the room, and had swallowed his porter before he had discovered that he had left his crutches behind him."

Such cases as these injure the really sick, particularly those whose symptoms are not very apparent.. Many prisoners adopt these schemes in order to get into hospital, where they get better food, less work, and have the chance of being with a favourite "pal."

Others will make themselves ill by swallowing tobacco, soap pills, or anything they know will make
them sick. There are others again who are afraid
to enter the hospital lest they should be poisoned
with a sleeping draught, or some other medicine
carelessly administered; and when they hear of any
sudden death in hospital they are ready to swear
" his light has been put out by the doctor." On the
other hand I have known it to happen that a prisoner went and complained to the doctor, who
roughly told him he was a " schemer," and the following week the prisoner was dead. Another time
a healthy looking old man, with chest disease, complained to the doctor of pain in that region. He
was dosed repeatedly with salts and senna—the
medicine for schemers—and in less than a fortnight
he was buried.

I could mention many cases similar to the above, and
also others where the prisoner was his own murderer
—if I may use the expression—but I will merely
mention one of them. The patient in this case was
afflicted with dropsy, and some affection of the heart.
He had been receiving two ounces of gin for a short
time, which he fancied was doing him good, and
being partial to that variety of medicine, he was
annoyed when it was ordered to be discontinued. Accordingly he resolved to make himself ill again, in
order to get the allowance of gin, and swallowed a large

piece of tobacco, which brought an increase to his heart complaint; and notwithstanding that the greatest attention was paid to his case by the doctor, before morning he was dead.

This prisoner lay in the next bed to mine, and among the many death-bed scenes I witnessed while in prison, I never saw one where the fear of death was so apparent, or the state of mind so appalling to the beholder.

The man had been a bully, and an avowed infidel. The prospect of death had now come upon him with awful suddenness. Fear and trembling took hold upon him, and as he thought of his past life, and the possible judgment seat, before which he might the next moment be summoned to appear, remorse and doubt seemed to torture him more than physical pain. At the closing scene he was evidently trying to believe, but could not, for he kept repeating, "If there be a God, if there be a God I hope He will forgive me; but I can't believe it, indeed I can't!" and so saying he expired.

Another death-bed scene impressed me much. The patient was paralysed in his lower extremities and could scarcely walk, but his general health appeared pretty good, and he was not confined to bed. He had a talent for mechanics and arithmetic, but a very bad temper and a very bad heart. His crime was sacrilege. In the next bed to his there lay a patient who was dying, and being in great pain was making a noise, which disturbed the studies and peace of mind of the other. A quarrel arose between the two on the subject. High words ensued. Curses, deep, black, loud, and long, soon followed, too soon for the officer to prevent, and there would certainly have been a fight if the dying man could have got out of bed, but the interference of the officer put an end to the disturbance. It was their parting words taken in connection with what followed, that made a deep impression upon me:—" If it wasn't that you are dying I would blacken your eyes for you," cried the mechanic. " How do you know I am dying ? You look as like dying as any-body, you miserable cripple," retorted the other. "Ah ! I'm tough stuff, you'll not see me die in a hurry." The cripple who uttered these words went shortly afterwards to bed, was seized with a paralytic affec-tion, which took the power of speech from him. He never uttered another syllable, but lay in bed for about a week, making frantic motions with his lips. I forget which of these two men died first, but they were buried together in the same grave.

Another death at this time excited a good deal of conversation among the prisoners. The patient had been tried under the Transportation Act, one of the bye-laws of which enacted that for every prison " report," or offence, the prisoner would lose one month of his remission. But convicts being usually punished under the most recent law, without reference to its being different from that under which they had received sentence, the prisoner I now refer to was sentenced to lose three months of his remission for one offence, that of having an inch or two of tobacco on his person. He had undergone nearly the whole of this additional punishment, when, only a few hours before his time came to leave the prison to meet his motherless children, for whom he seemed to have a very strong affection, he died suddenly of heart disease.

Some prisoners expired on the very day for their liberation. Some died screaming aloud that they were poisoned. Many died like the brutes, and a very few departed in peace, with a prayer on their lips. The great majority died as they had lived, and were forgotten by the spectators almost before their bodies had been laid in the grave.

CHAPTER VII.

AS a means of beguiling the time while in the hospital, I used to enter into long conversations with those of my fellow prisoners who were willing to gratify my curiosity, with a view of ascertaining their mode of life when out of prison. At first it was somewhat difficult for me to follow them in their talk, in consequence of their excessive use of " slang" terms; but in time I not only came to understand the nomenclature of thiefology, but also to use it fluently, as I found it more acceptable to my companions to do so, and rendered them more favourably disposed towards me.

One of my fellow prisoners was particularly communicative and obliging, and gave me a great deal of well-meant advice, no doubt, as to how I might live at the public expense *outside* the prison walls, as well as explanations in every department of crime. I remember the following dialogue taking place between us, which also serves to show how an ignoramus in the science, or a young country lad, perhaps for the first time convicted of crime, might be instructed

F

in vice, and incited to continue a career he had
perhaps very thoughtlessly, or under strong temptation, began.

"Harry," I asked, "what's that 'bloke'* here for,
who occupies the end bed?"

"Twineing."

"Twineing! What's that?"

"Don't you know that yet? why you must be a
greenhorn not to know that. Well! I'll tell you.
Suppose you start in the morning with a good
sovereign and a '*snyde*' † half-sovereign in your
pocket; you go into some place or other, and ask for
change of the sovereign, or you order some beer and
give the sovereign in payment; it's likely you will
get half-a-sovereign and silver back in change. Then
is the time to 'twine.' You change your mind, after
you have 'rung' ‡ your snyde half 'quid' § with the
good one, and throwing down the 'snyde' half, say
you prefer silver; the landlord or landlady, or whoever
it is, will pick up the snyde half-quid, thinking of
course it is the same one they had given you."

"Is that a good game, do you think?"

"Well, that depends on the party. If he has got
good 'togs' on, looks pretty decent, and can work it
well, he may make a good living at it."

"How much do you suppose?"

"If he can manage to begin every morning with

* Man.   † Counterfeit.   ‡ Substituted.   § Sovereign.

yellow stuff, he may make a couple of 'quid' a day ;
but if he can only muster white stuff, why of course
he can't make so much."

" Two pounds a day would do if it could be got
regularly, but I suspect there are not many who
make that ?"

" Oh ! I have known them make much more than
that, but of course it varies, some days nothing may
be done, but the great thing is to have something to
start with."

" Do you never think of trying to make money at
work ?"

" Work ! no, by jingo ! I'll never work ; that's
all they can make one do in prison, and it will be
time enough to work when we get there."

" I have heard you speak of 'hoisting,' how do
you go about that ?"

" Ah ! that's a much better game, but it requires a
fellow to be rigged out like a 'toff,'* and they generally have a 'flash moll,' † with them at that job.
She can secrete articles about her dress when in a
shop looking at things, and that's one way of 'hoisting.' Jewellers' shops are the best places for that
game. I know a bloke who made several hundreds at
it ; he took fine lodgings, and his moll looked quite
the lady, so he orders some jewellery to be sent on
sight ; he prigs the best of it and bolts. Then you can

* Gentleman. † Prostitute of the gayest sort.

F 2

get snyde jewellery made to look the same as real
stuff, and when you are in the shop with your moll,
she is trying on a ring perhaps, when you put the
snyde one in its place and she sticks to the right one."

"I am afraid that game would be above my
abilities ?"

"Well, I'll tell you what I did once, and what you
may do when you get out, when winter sets in ; you
can have some other game in summer, perhaps go
hawking, and do a bit of thieving when you see the
coast clear. My brother and I and another bloke
went out 'chance screwing,' one winter, and we
averaged three pounds a night each. My brother
had a spring cart and a fast trotting horse, so when
it began to grow dark, off we set to the outskirts of
London. I did the screwing in this way. Wherever
I saw a lobby lighted with gas, I looked in at the
key-hole. If I saw anything worth lifting I 'screwed'
the door—I'll teach you how to do it—seized the things,
into the cart with them, and off to the next place.
Now big Davey goes out about the same time as
you, and he knows a bloke with a cart, and so you
may do very well all winter at that game; but be
sure to leave off by nine o'clock as you would get ,it
very hot if caught after that time !"

"Well ! I shall see big Davey, perhaps, but don't
you think 'highflying' would suit me better, although
I know little about it ?"

"Oh! that's above your mark, a 'highflyer' is a bloke who dresses like a clergyman, or some gentleman. He must be educated, for his game is to know all the nobility and gentry, and visit them with got-up letters, and that kind of thing, for the purpose of getting subscriptions to some scheme. A church-building or missionary affair is the best game. There is only one good 'highflyer' in the prison. I knew him get 150*l.* from a gentleman in Devonshire once, and he thinks nothing of getting 30*l.* of a morning."

Finding my friend so communicative and apparently so experienced in the various branches of his profession, I took advantage of every convenient opportunity to ascertain from him the meaning of the slang terms which my comrades made use of when conversing together, but through ignorance of which I was often unable to understand exactly what they were talking about. On another occasion I accordingly asked him the meaning of a number of these terms which I had thus heard bandied about from time to time amongst them. On asking him about 'macing' he replied—

" Macing means taking an office, getting goods sent to it, and then 'bolting' with them ; or getting goods sent to your lodgings and then removing. I'll tell you a game that you might try now and again as you have a chance, and that is 'fawney dropping,' you

know ' fawney ' means a ring. Well, you must have
a 'pal,' and give him a ' snyde' ring with a ticket and
the price marked on it. When you are walking
along the street and see a likely ' toff' to buy the
ring, your ' pal' goes on before and drops it, you
come up behind him, and in front of the gentleman
you pick up the ring, which is ticketed, say five
pounds. Well, you turn to the ' toff' and say to him
that you have found a ring which is entirely useless
to you, as you never wear these articles, and ask him
to purchase it. He will most likely look at the
ticket, and see it marked five pounds, and if you
say you will let him have it for three pounds, or two
pounds, or even for one pound, if he hesitates, it is
also likely he will buy it, thinking he is getting a
great bargain."

"What do you mean by ' snow-dropping ?'" 1
asked.

"Oh !" said he, "that's a poor game. It means
lifting clothes off the bleaching line, or hedges.
Needy mizzlers, mumpers, shallow-blokes, and flats
may carry it on, but it's too low and paltry for
you."

"Who do you mean by mumpers and shallow-
blokes ?" I enquired.

" Why 'mumpers' are cadgers; beggars in fact.
There's old Dick over in that bed there; he used to
go 'mumping,' and when he got boosey with too

much lush he stole some paltry thing or other, and being so often convicted they have ' legged '* him at last. They can't make an honest living, and can't make a living by thieving; but, you know, it's different with you. You could make a fair thing by ' snotter-hauling,' even if you cannot get on at ' fly-buzzing,' which would suit you well enough; but it's better to stick to one good game, and get as expert at that as you can, for then you don't run so much risk, and you can keep a sharper look out after the ' coppers'.† Talking of mumping: old Dick used to go to the farm-houses with a piece of dried cow-dung, and ask for a bit of butter to put on it. Very often they took pity on him and gave him lots of meat; for they thought he must be very hungry to eat the cow-dung, which of course, you know, was only a dodge. In order to get to Liverpool once from some place up the Mersey, whence the fare down was a shilling, Dick went on board the steamer and asked the captain what he charged for lambs. ' A penny a-head,' says the captain. ' Oh! that will do,' says Dick; and away he goes among the passengers. When they were collecting the fares Dick holds out his penny, which was all the ' tin ' he had in the world. ' The fare's a shilling,' said the captain. ' Yes, it may be,' said Dick, ' but I asked you the fare for lambs. My name is Lamb; I'm an innocent crea-

* Sentenced. † Policemen.

ture, and the long and the short of it is I've only a
penny. If you can't take it, just give me a sail back
again.'   That chap over there with the one arm is a
regular 'mumper,' and he is a strong, robust fellow, able
to work with any man in the prison; but he can make
ten times more by ' mumping,' and I do not blame the
like of him going on that 'racket.' Every man for himself in this world. Do you see that little old man with
a cough on him ? Well, his game is 'needy-mizzling.'
He'll go out without a shirt, perhaps, and beg one
from house to house.   I have known him to get
thirty 'mill-togs '* in one day, which, at a 'bob' a-
piece, would fetch their thirty shillings. When he
can't go on that 'racket,' he'll turn ' mumper ' and
wood merchant (which means a seller of lucifer
matches) ; and sometimes he will take to rag and
bone collecting."

"What do you call a 'shallow-bloke ?' "

" He is a cove that acts the turnpike sailor; pretends he has been shipwrecked, and so on, or he
gets his arm bandaged, and put in a sling. I once
knew two blokes who went to an old captain's house
on that game, and as they were not able to reply to
some of his nautical questions, he and his son gave
them a regular horsewhipping. When they got
home they boasted to a lot of their ' chums ' how
much they had screwed out of the old captain. This

---

* Shirts.

induced some of them to go on the same 'racket,' and of course they met with the same warm reception. These 'shallow-blokes' turn 'duffers' sometimes. They get some 'duffing' silk hand-kerchiefs and cigars, and go about selling them for smuggled goods; or perhaps they will take to sing-ing in the streets. But I spoke of 'snotter-hauling.' Although I think you are too old for that 'racket' —and unless you were very hard up and in a crowd, I would not bother about it. It would not pay for the risk run. It does best for 'kids.'* A little boy can sneak behind a 'toff' and relieve him of his 'wipe' as easily as possible. I know a little fellow who used to make seven 'bob' a-day at it on the average ; but there were more silk 'wipes' used then than there are now."

"What do you mean by 'lob-sneaking,' and 'Peter-screwing ?' "

"Why, 'lob' means the till, and 'Peter' means a safe. Stealing the till and opening the safe is what we call "lob-sneaking and Peter-screwing."

"And what is 'jumping' and 'jilting?'

"'Jumping' is getting into a house through the window ; and 'jilting' is getting in on the sly, or on false pretences at the door, and sneaking what you can find. It's not a bad game to go into hotels, for instance, as a traveller, and as soon as you see a

* Boys.

·chance to sneak anything, to bolt with it. I know some fellows who make a fair living in this way."

" Then there is 'twisting' and 'fencing?' "

"When you go into any place where hats, coats, or umbrellas are left in the lobby, you can take a new ' tog,' or a new hat, by mistake for your own. That is 'twisting,' or ringing the changes. Then the 'fence-master' is the fellow who buys stolen property. I will give you the names of some of these blokes in London before you go out. You must know where to dispose of a ' super,'* or whatever you get, or it would be of no use to you. You know what ' buzzing,' or pocket-picking is, of course ; and you have heard of working on the 'stop,' most likely. Which means picking pockets when the party is standing still ; but it is more difficult on the 'fly.' You must remember that. I remember once going along Oxford Street, and I prigged an old woman's ' poke,'† on the 'fly.' She missed it very quick, and was coming after me when I slipped it into an old countryman's pocket as I was passing. She came up and accused me with stealing her purse. I, of course, allowed her to search me, and asked her to fetch a 'bobby,' if she was not satisfied. Well, I followed the old countryman and accused him of stealing my purse. And, my Crikey ! if you had only seen how the old codger looked when he

* Watch.   † Purse.

found the purse in his pocket. I threatened to give him in charge of the first 'copper' I saw; and he was so frightened that I actually got a 'quid' out of him to let him off."

" Well now, tell me about 'snyde-pitching."

"Snyde, you know, means counterfeit or bad, anything bad we call snydey. Snyde-pitching is passing bad money; and is a capital racket, especially if you can get rid of 'fins.' "

" What are ' fins ?' "

"Five pound notes, or flash notes. I can give you the address of one or two fellows who make bad coins, and you can pass one or two when you see a fair chance."

" What do they charge for sovereigns, for instance ?"

" The charge depends on the quality, you can get them at from six to fifteen shillings. Those at fifteen shillings no one can discover. They are the weight, the size, and all that is required. The low-priced ones of course you. must run more risk with. Making bad coins is one of the best games out, and you can carry it on with less risk. For instance you can have your place where you work so blocked up that before anyone can enter, you will have time to destroy all your dies and tools; and melt or 'plant' your metal, and without them they cannot convict you. I know a bloke in Birmingham now, who was getting up Scotch one pound notes when I was 'copt,' and he is a capital hand at the trade. He once made a good deal by making snyde postage stamps."

"But one would require to know something about the different metals before they could be able to make 'snyde.'"

"Yes, that is necessary, but I think I know who will tell you. He has got twenty years, and is not likely to get a chance of doing more at the trade. These fellows who follow that racket are rather close, and don't want to tell anyone."

"The other day I heard a bloke talking about a 'picking-up moll' he used to live with. What did he mean by that?"

"O! that's a very common racket. He meant a 'flash-tail,' or prostitute who goes about the streets at nights trying to pick up 'toffs.' When she manages to do this her accomplice the coshman (a man who carries a 'cosh' or life preserver) comes up, when she has signed to him that she has got the 'toff's' watch and chain, and quarrels with him for meddling with his wife. Whilst the quarrel is going on the moll walks off with the booty. I know one coshman who pretends to be a missionary, and wears a white choker. Instead of quarrelling, he talks seriously to the 'toff' about the sin of fornication, and advises him to pursue a more becoming life in future, and finishes off by giving him a religious tract!"

"Now I have nearly finished my questions, but whilst there is time tell me about 'magging,' and 'mag-flying.'"

"Magging is not so good a game as it used to be. It means more particularly, swindling a greenhorn out of his cash by the mere gift of the gab. You know if it were not for the flats, how could the sharps live? You can 'mag' a man at any time you are playing cards or at billiards, and in various other ways. As for 'mag-flying,' that is not good for much. You have seen those blokes at fairs and races, throwing up coppers, or playing at pitch and toss? Well these are 'mag-flyers.' The way they do it is to have a penny with two heads or two tails on it, which they call a 'grey,' and of course they can easily dupe flats from the country."

"How do they call it a 'grey,' I wonder?"

"I suppose they have named it after Sir George Grey, because he is a two-faced bloke."

"Well then tell me about 'locusing,' and 'bellowsing.'"

"Locusing is putting a chap to sleep with chloroform, and bellowsing is putting his light out. In other words, drugging and murder."

"Now then, shew me how to hang a fellow up, or put the 'flimp' on him, as you call it."

"D'ye see that bone in the wrist? Just get that on the windpipe—so," (shewing me practically how to garotte). While at this interesting experiment we heard a voice cry, " Cheese it, cheese it, Harry! there's the 'Screw' looking at you !" which warned us that the prison warder was also taking notes, and my lesson for that day came to a rather abrupt conclusion.

CHAPTER VIII.

ANOTHER COMPANION—A CAREER OF CRIME—HIS OPINIONS ABOUT
RELIGION AND CHURCH RATES—AN INCURABLE—HIS OPINION ABOUT
FLOGGING.

ANOTHER of my companions in hospital gave me the particulars of his history in answer to my enquiries. I give them precisely in his own words:—

"I was about fifteen years of age before I stole any money, or got into any trouble; but I used to 'nick' little things, such as fruit, &c., when I was a kid. My father kept a small shop, but I was bound an apprentice to a very peculiar branch of the Sheffield trade; and before I had finished my apprenticeship I committed my first crime. I was playing at bagatelle one night, and lost all my cash, and as I was anxious to win it back, I broke into my master's premises, and took all the money that was in the cash-box. I got 'copt,' and was sent into the county jail. When I came out I enlisted in the army. My father bought me off after I had been in the regiment a short time. I then took to hawking, but I did not make much money at that, so I enlisted again,—deserted, and got flogged; and the flogging

made me a blackguard;—committed another crime,
and got out of the army. Afterwards I committed
other crimes, and was at last copt and sentenced to
five years' penal servitude. I was sent to do most of
it at Gibraltar. After coming home I resolved I
should make a fair trial to gain an honest livelihood. I had about thirteen pounds of a gratuity
coming to me, and by the aid of the vicar I got all
that at once, and set up as a greengrocer. But as I
was not very well acquainted with the business I soon
lost my little capital, and I resolved to try and get
work at my trade. I called on all the 'gaffers' in
that business, but none of them would employ me.
Those who knew me would have nothing to do with
me; those who didn't wanted a character, which of
course I could not give. Well, I went two days
without tasting a bit of food; but on the third I
ate some turnips. On the fourth day I became so
desperate with hunger that I determined on going
on the 'cross.' I commenced, and committed seven-
teen burglaries right off, in various parts of the
country. The first was in my own town, and the
moment I got the 'wedge'* 'planted†' I went to the
police-office and asked for a bed for the night, as I
had no money. Next day, early, there was a great
hubbub about my job. One of the police came to
the office and swore it must have been done by me;

* Silver-plate.　　　　　　　† Hidden.

but when the superintendent told him that I had slept in the station-house all night, and that it could not have been me, he never said any more about it. The next place I robbed was a church; but all the rest were shops. I was tried for the church and two of the other jobs; but I got off the former, as the clergyman prosecuted me, when it ought to have been some other official connected with it. I pleaded guilty to the second charge against me; and it's that I'm now here for. When I was in prison, waiting for trial, I called myself a Roman Catholic, and was visited by the priest. One day I confessed to him that I had robbed a church, and that I was very sorry for it—and so I was, upon my word. That's the only crime I ever committed which gave me any trouble. Well, the priest was thunderstruck, and looked daggers at me; but when I told him it was a Protestant church, he gave me absolution, and said the crime was not so bad as he at first thought."

"What religion do you profess now?" I enquired.

"Well, I'm down in the books now as a Protestant, or Church of England man; but I do not believe all that churchmen believe. I think there's a good deal of humbug about what is called Christianity altogether. I have tried several creeds, and there's none of them squares exactly with my ideas."

"Which of them have you tried?"

"I was eighteen months a Mormon. My uncle is

G

an elder in their church; but I got enough of them one night at a meeting. After the business was concluded, one of the members proposed that the lights should be put out during the remainder of the proceedings.—My Crikey! that night was enough for me. . . . . . I was in earnest at first though; and when I was baptised and anointed, I intended to have gone out to the settlement in America."

"What do you object to in the Church of England?"

"Oh! I don't pay much attention to these matters. I like a good man, no matter what church he belongs to. For instance, the Presbyterian minister at 'Gib.' was a first-rate man; and so is that chaplain at Pentonville, the Rev. Mr. Sherman. But I am of the barber's opinion about church-rates."

"What was his opinion?"

"Well, a certain barber opened a shop down our way, and shortly afterwards was called on to pay the church-rates. 'Church-rates,' says he, 'what have I to do with church-rates? I never go near the church. I belong to the dissenters.' 'Well, but you know the church is always open to receive you, and every Sunday the doors are open for you to come and worship; and you ought to consider it a privilege to be permitted to attend on the ministration of God's Holy Word,' was the reply. 'I do not consider it a privilege to go to a church I don't believe in,' said the barber. 'I go to a different church, which I am

pleased with, and therefore I won't pay you any rates.
'But you know the law will compel you to pay them.'
'Oh, then, there they are; if the law says so, it must
be done.' 'Well, as you have paid me so promptly
I shall be a regular customer of yours, and will now
have a 'shave' and my hair cut,' said the collector. He
only continued for a short time, however, to patronize
the barber, having found a shop nearer home and
more convenient. But at the end of the year the
barber made out his account all the same as if he had
continued his custom as he had promised to do.
When the collector got the account, he said, 'How's
this? I don't owe you a quarter of this sum; you
must have made a mistake. I have only been so
many times at your shop altogether, and yet you
charge me as if I had gone all the year round.'
'My dear sir," replied the barber, 'you know that
my shop, as by law established, is always open to
receive you, excepting Sunday, when your shop is
open, so that you may avail yourself of my skill, and
you ought to consider it a very great privilege to be
permitted to do so.' 'I don't consider it any privilege to get that from you which I can get from
others that I happen to prefer, on the same terms,
and therefore I refuse to pay your account.' 'Then,
it appears, I am obliged to pay your account whatever it may be, whether I get value for it or not, but
yet you are not obliged to pay me mine unless you

G 2

do get value for it, even when you promise to take value. Good morning.' 'Good morning,' said the collector ; and the barber retired.

" You will see from this colloquy what the barber's notions were about church rates. Now, I have an idea that it is most unjust for one set of religious men to force their neighbours who differ from them, to help to pay for the support of their church, particularly when they are able themselves to do all that is required in that way, if they were willing. This mainstay and foundation being rotten, the fabric cannot be secure. The churchman acts unjustly in this, and to act unjustly is anti-christian : therefore the churchman is no Christian any more than I am a Dutchman."

" Well, we'll leave the church question at present. Have you anything more to tell me about yourself ? Have you never thought seriously about changing your mode of life when you get out of prison again ? An intelligent fellow like you would do well in America, and I would strongly recommend you to leave the country as soon as you get your liberty."

" As to altering my conduct, I tell you that when I was in the separate cells, I did resolve on it, and began to pray and read good books, but after I got among the other prisoners I gave it all up again ; I should like to go abroad well enough, but I shall not have funds for it, so I must stop at home."

" Then do you intend to go thieving and robbing again ?"

" Well, I shall never go another day without food, that's certain. If I can get it honestly, good and well; if not I'll steal: why should a man starve in a Christian country ?"

" You have the workhouse to go to."

" The workhouse ! it's a second jail : I would nearly as soon be in prison, and when you have a chance of getting off without being caught, it's better to run the risk and chance it, for all the difference there is or ever can be between the workhouse and the prison. They can't make a man work unless they feed and clothe him, any more than they can make a steam engine go without fuel. Well, give me food and I'll work ; work is no punishment to me, if I can get meat to support it, and if I don't I can't, that's all about it. But what's the good of making me work for years, at work that will not be of any use to me when I get out ? I have only learnt one trade, there are only a very few men in that trade, they won't employ me; then what am I to do ? Starve in a Christian country ? It isn't likely ; and as for the workhouse, I shall never go to it as long as I can be fed in prison, with the chance always of keeping out of both ?"

" Suppose they should flog you next time ?"

" In the first place, I have a disease on me now

that would prevent me from being flogged, so that I have no fear of flogging. But, even if I was able to stand flogging, all the difference it would make to me, would be to make me keep a sharper eye after the ' coppers.' Small game would not then tempt me so much. I should look after larger stakes, go in at heavier jobs, and calculate well my chances of escape before going to work. Once I had made up my mind to commit a crime, and saw the coast clear, the chance of all the floggings in the world would not deter me. I'll find you fellows in the prison to-day who will take a good round flogging for a pound of tobacco! now do you think that the mere chance of the lash would hinder these men from attempting to get hold of a few hundred pounds' worth of jewellery? It's not likely. Thieves weren't frightened into honesty by the gallows, nor would they be now, if they were to be cut into mince-meat. Thousands might be led into honest ways if suitable work was found for them, but it would require to be very different work from that of the ' navvy,' and then many of them have to be *learned* to work before they could make a living at all."

"Then you don't think flogging did you any good at all?"

" Certainly it did not; and what's more, you will never find a man doing much good after being flogged. It either makes him an invalid, or a desperado. It may make him quiet under authority, but it ensures the very opposite when he is free."

This prisoner was a more than usually clever and intelligent type of a numerous class of convicts—not the most difficult class to cure, but the next to it, perhaps. Unlike the city-bred professional thief, he had been taught to work, and such work as he could perform was no punishment to him. Unlike the professional, he goes out of the prison hesitating, wavering, as to his future course : willing to take work if suitable; determined to avoid the workhouse; easily tempted to steal, resolved to do so rather than starve; but, on the whole, anxious to make a comfortable livelihood. He had one son, and I remember well how glad he was when some benevolent person wrote to him to say that he had been bound an apprentice to a respectable trade. He is now dead. Another of my companions was of a somewhat different class, and a much more difficult subject to deal with. He told me that he was fifty-seven years of age. I asked him how long he had been a prisoner, not adding his sentences together, but how long he had actually been in prison.

" Thirty-seven years," he replied.

" How old were you when you got into trouble first ?"

" Fourteen."

" What was your first sentence ?"

"Seven years' transportation."

"How did you like Australia?"

"Well, the place is well enough, and a man can get a living easier abroad than he can at home. But I have been rather a queer customer in my time. I don't believe there's a man in this prison, or in any prison, who has gone through more hardships and punishments than I have done."

"Were you ever flogged?"

"Flogged! I should think I have. Just wait until night, when I am going to bed, and I'll let you see my back all in ridges with the cat."

"What effect had the flogging on your conduct?"

"Flogging takes out one devil and puts in seven. That's the effect it had on me. But there's not one in a hundred could stand the floggings and punishments I have endured. I had ten years once in Australia, and I was in the penal class most of the time, and, by jingo! they know how to punish there."

".Suppose I were to offer you 20*l*. to be flogged, would you accept the money and take the flogging?"

"I should think I would, and that very quick, too. I would as soon take a bashing as bread and water for seven days."

"Then a bashing, as you call it, would not frighten you from committing a crime?"

"If I thought I was going to be caught even, I should not commit a crime. A 'flat' or a 'mumper' may do a job to get into prison, but I never do anything unless I believe I am to escape. It's the getting caught, that's the crime, the punishment you have got to chance. A fellow needn't begin thieving if he is to be frightened at punishment; he would never make a living at it. It requires a fellow with a good heart to be a thief, I can tell you; and if his heart is not in the right place, he'd better keep on the square."

"Now, tell me; do you never think seriously about your evil ways? You are getting up in years, and although you appear to be very robust in your general health at present, you cannot expect to live very much longer in this world."

"Well, to tell you the truth, I do sometimes think of leading an honest life. But I am so hardened now to all punishment that I don't care very much what I do. It's not easy for a man at my age to change all of a sudden to be a Christian, and then it's so difficult to get work suitable for one's abilities, that I am almost driven to go on the cross. I have a very good brother, who has been very kind to me, and I've been thinking several times of going home and getting work from him. He is the only man who ever did me a kindness since I was fourteen years of age, and I love and respect him very much."

This man had been longer in prison than any other I met with. He had been five times a convict. I considered him the very worst of a certain class of prisoners that I ever knew, and feel quite convinced that he will not be many weeks out of prison. He was constantly trafficking with his fellow-prisoners, and when he could get a chance to steal, his hands *would* be at work. I remember his being in the cook-house for a time, and almost every day he stole several pounds of mutton or beef. He would steal anything for an inch of tobacco. He was turned out of the cook-house on suspicion, but they never could punish him for theft except on one occasion, which happened in the following manner.

The prisoners were in the habit of getting a pint of oatmeal gruel for supper. This pint of gruel was supposed to contain two ounces of meal; but in order to make it part better it was made thinner, so that every night there was a surplus. This surplus the prisoners thought belonged to them, and some of the officers permitted the orderlies for the day, who served it out, to divide whatever remained amongst the prisoners in their own wards. The authorities, however, did not allow the prisoners more than a pint :—no matter whether it was thick or thin, no matter whether there was only one ounce of meal in it, back to the cook-house and the swill-tub the surplus must go. Some officers adhered to the rule, others did not. The officer in charge of the prisoner referred to was one of those who did, and when

my friend helped himself to a pint out of the surplus
gruel he was " reported " the same evening (which happened to be a Saturday). On Sunday the governor,
departing from his usual custom, came to his cell,
and passed sentence on him there. When the prisoner came out of ' Chokey,' as the punishment cells
are called by the prisoners, he came to me about the
Sunday sentence of a hungry man for taking a pint of
gruel, which in some proportion belonged to himself.
He fancied it was not legal to pass sentence on a
Sunday, and thought he might get back the time he
had forfeited, by appealing to the director. I told him
I did not approve of the conduct of the governor,
but at the same time expressed the opinion that the
director would not interfere in his case. (Whether he
did so or not I am unable to say, as I was removed
before the director's visit was due.) This prisoner
was a big stout man, above thirteen stone weight,
and there was nothing the matter with him except a
diseased leg. This leg was rather a convenience to
him than otherwise. If he disliked any work he was
put to, he could always get rid of it by making his leg
sore, and this could not be prevented, nor brought
directly home to him. When he was at Dartmoor
prison he was always in hospital ; but now, as his work
pleased him better he seldom troubled the doctor.
On the contrary, when about due to go home, that is
when he arrived at his last stage, and became entitled

to beer and other privileges, he wanted to get out of
the invalid prison, where these privileges are not
allowed unless the state of the invalid requires them,
and to be sent to the public works where they would
be granted.

Many convicts are so afflicted that they can almost
compel the doctor to admit them into the hospital.
So whenever they are put into some billet they like
they are well, and whenever they are put into one
they dislike they send in a sick report, and the
medical officer in general must admit them. This
was the case with the prisoner I have referred to.
Moreover, I question if he was ever a single day in
the prison without doing something that was considered wrong, and yet he was very seldom detected
or punished. Every day he was trafficking, frequently
he was stealing, and he told lies as a rule. Speaking
the truth was quite an exceptional matter with him.
Thieves generally consider it to be a virtue rather
than a sin to tell a lie to save a 'pal' from punishment, but in cases where their own interests are not
specially at stake, they can speak the truth as well as
other men. But this prisoner seemed utterly in-
capable of speaking the truth, even when falsehood
brought no advantage to him.

CHAPTER IX.

ANOTHER PRISONER—"HAPPY AS A KING"—CURE OF A DOCTOR—THE
TOBACCO AND FOOD EXCHANGE—ANOTHER JAIL-BIRD—CIVIL AND
LAZY—UNDESERVED REMISSION—PRISON DIRECTORS, AND HOW THEY
DISCHARGE THEIR DUTIES—I PETITION TO GO ABROAD ON "INSUFFI-
CIENT GROUNDS."

ANOTHER prisoner I knew had been about thirty-two years in prison—he was paralyzed, and if he had been allowed a little tobacco daily, would have been as happy as a king, and never sought to leave the prison. He generally sold most of his food to other prisoners for tobacco; occasionally he was detected and punished, and I always observed that he came out of 'Chokey' fatter than when he went in. Neither was his an exceptional case in this respect. The penal diet, which mainly consists of farinaceous food, will keep up the flesh, though not the strength, as well as the regular diet. In Scotland I have seen prisoners get stout in appearance on the oatmeal! but on the other hand they generally broke out in boils, after being six or nine months without other varieties of food; and I have also known very stout men lose two or three stone in weight in as many

months. I am inclined to believe that tobacco is
beneficial in cases of insufficient food. I do not use
it myself, nor do I think it beneficial to those who
have plenty of food, but the reverse. I have known
prisoners, however, who had good health in the Scotch
prisons, when they used tobacco—and fortunately for
them, the weed and many other luxuries are easily
obtained there, if you only know the way and have
money. If I had known at the commencement of
my prison career what I now know, I might have had
mutton chops daily, if I had been inclined to adopt
some of the ' lodges' I afterwards learnt. I knew
one prisoner who obtained his end in a somewhat
questionable way. He had made some complaint to
the doctor, who, as usual, paid very little attention to
it. On seeing that he was not to receive any
medical aid by fair means, he resorted to foul, and
took up a certain utensil, full to the brim, and emptied
its contents in the face and over the shirt-front of the
hapless pill-compounder. The remedy was doubtless
severe, but the disease was chronic and the improvement marked and rapid. The prisoner got good diet
and was soon after in good health."

The price of tobacco at the "Thieves' Palace or
Invalid Criminal Hotel," for so the Surrey Prison was
sometimes designated by the inmates, was about one
shilling per ounce, when I left. It seldom went
below 10*d.* At first when I arrived, there were yards

of it in one place or another, but the crime of having
a bit of it found on the person, being now severely
punished, the convicts keep it out of sight more
carefully and are more on their guard, seldom having
more on their person than they can swallow. All
'fly' men who use tobacco can procure it in any convict prison; but the 'flats,' have to deny themselves
the prisoners' greatest luxury, but even they sometimes get a taste of it by selling their food. An inch
of tobacco will fetch four ounces of cheese, or
mutton, it will also procure one and a-half pounds
of bread. Sometimes it is worth more, according to
the business abilities of the trader. The exchange
of food is a daily custom. One prisoner with a good
appetite requiring double the allowance of food, will
give four ounces of cheese for twenty-three ounces
of bread, or five ounces of mutton for the same
quantity. In this way the man with the capacious
stomach gets it filled, and the man with a dainty
appetite gets better food. All this sort of traffic is
quite contrary to the prison rules, and in the case of
tobacco it is severely punished, but prisoners will
have it, and many of them do have it regularly.
The prisoner referred to at the commencement of
this chapter was remarkable for his love of the weed,
and it was not often he missed a day without getting
a taste of it, at the sacrifice, however, of nearly all
his food. He was only fit for the jail or the work-

house, and would commit a theft rather than deny himself a single meal."

" I will mention only another of my companions in hospital, whose case will illustrate with what wisdom and discrimination the prison directors and governors use the powers delegated to them, encouraging the well-behaved and reforming the penitent convict !"

This prisoner had been a long time a convict. I asked him when he was first convicted.

"In 1838," he replied.

"What sentence did you then receive ?"

" I got two sentences, one seven years and the other eight years, making fifteen together, and I did about seven years and eight months out of the fifteen years.

"You got a free pardon, I suppose ?"

" Yes."

"Did they not send you abroad, then ?"

"My health was not very strong and I did my time at the ships."

" How did you like them ?"

" Oh, very well, there was not so much of this stupid humbugging-us-about system as there is now, but we were not kept so clean. The Scots-greys were frequently on the march on the clothes of the convicts."

" What was your next sentence ?"

" Life."

" How many years did you have to do ?"

"I got off on 'medical grounds' when I had done about two years and a-half. I got 'copt' again, however, and was sent back to do 'life' a second time; then I was liberated after I had done seven and a-half years more, making ten years altogether out of two 'life's.'"

" What have you got this time ?"

" Ten years."

" What do you intend to do when you get out this time ?"

" Why, it's no use trying to get work ; I am not able for anything very hard now, and I think I shall make snyde half-crowns."

" You'll get caught again if you commence that game."

" No I won't. I did that when I was out last, and several times before, and I have never been caught yet for that job. I can go and buy silver spoons, and get tools that I can destroy in a few minutes."

" But why not go to the workhouse ?"

" The workhouse ! why, the workhouse in our country is as bad, if not worse than this, and this is bad enough. No; I will never enter a workhouse as long as I can get anything to steal. Some workhouses are better than this ; but then when you steal you are not always caught, and you have your-

H

self to blame if you're 'copt.' I will steal the very
first chance I get, as soon as I get out at the gates.
They won't give me work I can make a living at,
and I'll not starve nor want a single meal. I'll have
better mutton the day I get out than we have here,
perhaps, and it will cost me nothing."

This prisoner was a thorough jail-bird, quiet and
civil to his officers, growling at his food, slow at work,
but always doing a little—a very good example of
the type "civil and lazy." He received his ten
years' sentence about four years ago, when it was
customary for those who had revoked a licence to be
refused a remission of sentence a second time. But,
in September, 1864, he was credited with two-and-a-
half years' remission, and in the summer of 1865 he
was credited with another three months, unasked,
unexpected, and in the latter case, quite inexplicable
consistently with justice to others. Indeed, the only
explanation which can be given of this undeserved
and unexpected leniency is to suppose that the prison
officials, like shopkeepers, treat their " regular "
customers best, and that they do not see any reason
why their business should not be encouraged, and
the prisons kept as full and quiet as possible by the
same methods as other men adopt who have to make
an honest living by their trade. We have seen the
effects of cotton famine, and I am sure matters
would have come to a sad pass if we were to witness

a *convict famine,* and to be compelled to open our workhouse gates to the starving families of our convict guardians.

It is very natural, and in a sense, laudable, that these latter should seek by such means as are available to them to prevent the occurrence of any such calamity. Hence, civil quiet ruffians, like the prisoner I have referred to, are encouraged. They are an article with which they have little trouble, and out of which they can make both profit and capital.

My own case was somewhat different. Once out of prison I was not likely to return ; neither was I of the " sort " prison officials are accustomed to manage. Moreover, my eyes were open, and my future was not quite so certainly in their hands as to warrant them in feeling secure that what I saw might not hereafter be described for the information of others. The difficulties I experienced in gaining even the slightest concession were great, and contrast strangely with the case I have mentioned. A few months previous to my discharge from hospital, I gave in my name in the usual manner as being desirous to speak with the visiting director. I may here explain that there are four directors of convict prisons in England. One of them had the manners and the reputation of a gentleman ; two of them may indeed have been men of ability, but their de-

H 2

portment to the convicts was certainly not calculated
to give them any more exalted ideas than they
already possessed of the civility and good manners
obtaining amongst those above them ; the fourth
was the beau ideal of a bully, and his influence on
the convict the statistics of the prison will show to
have been baneful in the extreme.

The powers of these directors are much more ex-
tensive than that of the magistrates in our county
prisons. In the latter, the visiting magistrate will
ask the prisoners if they have any complaint to make ;
but this is not the case with the convict director,
whom none can approach without giving formal
notice, and who generally leaves the prison followed
by the curses and maledictions of the majority of
the prisoners. In reality, the prison director holds
absolute sway over some thousands of his fellow
men ; there is no appeal from his decisions ; his court
is held, and prisoners are sentenced and punished,
but there are no reporters for the press. The whole-
some influence of public opinion does not penetrate
that secret and irresponsible tribunal. Such being
the case, it is to be lamented that we cannot or do
not find men to fill the office who are capable of dis-
charging its duties with fairness and civility. Before
I sought an interview with the director, I had written
a letter to the late Mr. Cobden, in which, after nar-
rating the particulars of my case, I expressed the

hope that he might feel it consistent with his public duty to endeavour to procure for me the same treatment with reference to liberation as had been extended to other prisoners who had suffered the loss of a similar limb at the same prison before me. This was considered improper language, and the letter was suppressed. When called before the authorities on this occasion, I asked them to point out all the objectionable passages, in order that I might know what to omit in writing it another time. But this they would not do, and all the satisfaction I could get was that my letter might not only be shown to the Home Secretary, but also be noticed in the House of Commons, and that they might be blamed for passing it. The idea of my letter being noticed in the House of Commons was new and not very agreeable to me, but I also thought it very improbable that such would be the case, and remarked in reply that there was nothing in the letter that a prisoner could be justly blamed for writing, and that its publication could not have an injurious effect on the public interest. This was not denied, but the letter was suppressed nevertheless, and I presume, still lies among many similar documents which have from time to time met with the same fate.

On the morning following my application for an interview with the director, I was informed that I could not see him on that occasion, as he was expected that very day. This refusal appeared strange to me, inasmuch as I knew of other prisoners who were permitted to speak to the director who had not given in their names earlier than I did. There was nothing for it, however, but to wait patiently for another month, and to give in my name a second time, when I was permitted my first interview with a prison director. I remember it well.

The director was seated at a desk in the governor's room, with the governor likewise seated at his side. A large book lay on the desk, in which the director wrote, or was supposed to write, what the prisoners requested or complained of, what punishments he awarded, with all the particulars regarding the offences, what answers he gave to complaints, requests, &c. Not a very trustworthy book that, I should say. In front of the desk stood two warders with staves in their hands, and between these two men I was placed. I asked the director, very politely, if he would be kind enough to look into my case, and recommend me to the Home Secretary for the same leniency as had been extended to other three prisoners, who had each lost a leg in prison from disease, shortly before me.

" No prisoners have lost their legs from disease ; there was some accident connected with it."

This was the reply made to me, in a gruff, bullying tone of voice. I then begged his pardon, and com-

menced to give the names of the prisoners whose
cases I had mentioned. But when the director saw
that I was familiar with the cases he would not permit me to proceed, and refused peremptorily to look
into my case. I then asked him to be kind enough
to allow me to petition the Home Secretary on the
merits of my case, as I petitioned the first time solely
on the ground of having lost my leg, and being in
bad health.

"No, no, no! that will do. Call the next man."

And I was bundled out of the room, with the
prayer on my lips that I might never more be compelled to speak to such a man. Convicts, I may
add, are freely permitted to petition the Home Secretary every twelve months; at this time nearly
eighteen months had elapsed since I petitioned first.
To show that I had some grounds for my request,
I will mention the cases of the prisoners who had
lost limbs at the same prison shortly before me.

A.—Sentence nearly double mine. Crime, rape
on his own daughter. He had only been a short
time in prison when his leg required to be
amputated, in consequence of disease in the
knee-joint. He was told by the doctor, before
the operation, that he would be liberated on
recovery. Patient died.

B.—A regular thief, with many previous convictions.
Lost a diseased limb. Was offered his liberty

by the authorities, and his license was issued,
but his father would not receive him. He
ultimately died in prison.

C.—A French housebreaker who had been in
English prisons before. Sentence, seven years.
Lost his leg in consequence of disease in the
knee-joint, and recovered speedily. He was
sent home a few months after the operation,
and before he had been so long in prison as I
had been at the time of my request.

I now felt rather unhappy under the severity with
which I was treated, and wrote a letter to my brother,
in which I mentioned having seen the visiting director; but this letter was also suppressed, and I
was warned not to mention the director's name in
any letter, or inform my friends of the suppressed
letter to Mr. Cobden. I felt hurt at its suppression,
for its spirit was most unobjectionable; and the
governor seemed to think so too, for he allowed me
a sheet of paper to write to the director. My object
in this letter was to obtain permission to petition the
Home Secretary for liberty to go abroad. At this time
all healthy and sound prisoners of my age, who had
received the same sentence, were about due for their
"ticket," in Western Australia; and as I did not
see why the loss of a leg should cause me to be kept
in prison for years after they were liberated, I resolved to petition to go abroad. I accordingly wrote

my letter to the director, carefully excluding any reference to my treatment in the government prison, so as not to give any offence. An answer came back, in suspicious haste, that I was to petition the Home Secretary in the very same language as I had used in the letter. I was not exactly pleased with this, as I wished to say something about the merits of my case ; but there was no help for it, and I must petition as I was told, or not petition at all. I petitioned accordingly, in precisely the same language, merely using the third instead of the first person singular. But it was of no use. Indeed I do not believe the petition was ever sent to the Secretary of State at all. All these documents go in the first instance to the directors, and they are understood to deal with them as they think proper.

Sometimes their machinery gets out of order, and the method by which these things are done gets to be exposed. Two cases where answers were received to petitions *which were never sent*, are very familiar to the majority of convicts. In the one case the prisoner had drawn his paper, but delayed writing the petition. The reply came notwithstanding, " Not sufficient grounds." In the other case the petition was discovered mislaid in the office, or some other part of the prison, after the prisoner had received his answer. The official replies to petitions appear to be stereotyped, and the names of the petitioners are merely written on the margin. One reply does for any number of petitions, and all the officials have to do is to write the name of the prisoner who draws petition paper on the margin of the answer, about a month after the paper has been issued. On the day I wrote the last petition I was discharged from the hospital, and transferred down-stairs to a room containing twenty-four prisoners.

CHAPTER X.

MY readers must now descend with me from the hospital, to what the convicts termed the twenty-four bedded room in the prison. In the cells and in the hospital, quietness reigned, but in the twenty-four bedded room it was different. Here the prisoners talked and conducted themselves very much as they felt inclined, and in the evenings the noise and tumult was sometimes beyond description. The inmates were constantly changing, some going up-stairs to hospital, some coming from it, and every now and again there were fresh arrivals from other prisons. The daily routine observed here and in the similar wards was as follows :—

We started out of bed at half-past five a.m., summer and winter; washed, dressed, and made our beds, and two or three times every week assisted in scrubbing the floor. At six o'clock the officer opened the room door and counted us. At half-past six we had

breakfast. About twenty minutes past seven we were
ranked up in the corridor, and counted a second time.
At half-past seven we were in chapel. At eight o'clock
we were on parade and counted a third time. Those
who worked outside and were receiving full diet went
to their work. Those who worked inside walked on
the parade until half-past eight. They were then
ranked up and counted for the fourth time; and
at nine o'clock all were at work. At 11·45 we were
counted for the fifth time, and at twelve o'clock
we were at dinner. At 12·50 we were again ranked
in the corridor and counted for the sixth time. At
one o'clock we were on parade and counted for the
seventh time, before exercise commenced. At ten
minutes after two we were counted for the eighth
time, and at two we were all again at work. When
we left off work in the evening we were counted for
the ninth time, amongst the party with whom we
worked, and for the tenth time when we returned to
the ward. At half-past five we got supper, and at half-
past seven we were ordered to bed. At eight o'clock we
were commanded to cease talking, and at nine o'clock
the night officer counted us for the eleventh time
and left us to repose. I used to rejoice when bed-
time came, for I then could be alone and at home.
Then there were no prison walls for me, for I had
ceased brooding over the past, and endeavoured to
peer into and prepare for the uncertain future. In

winter and spring, when the weather was cold, it used
to be rather trying for me to stand so long on parade
being counted. About an hour or an hour-and-a-
half was spent in this way each day. Then the
clothing of those of us who worked indoors was the
same on the coldest day in winter as on the hottest
day in summer. This was an excellent arrangement
for keeping the hospital supplied with patients. I
knew many who suffered from this cause, and some
who attributed their death to the want of proper
under-clothing. I felt the cold more perhaps than
the others, as my hands were exposed holding my
crutches, and my speed in walking could never get
beyond that of a goods train, whilst my companions
could run at express speed when it suited them.

My employment was knitting and reading aloud to
the prisoners. At that time, and up to a very recent
date, it was the custom where fifty or a hundred
prisoners were at work, for one of the prisoners to
read aloud an hour every forenoon and afternoon.
When I commenced this reading, my audience were
very careless about listening, unless when I read
some amusing work of fiction. Indeed, other
prisoners did not attempt to read any book of a more
solid description. But during the years I was
engaged in this way I had the most abundant
and satisfactory testimony that I had obtained an
influence over the minds of the prisoners, and had

succeeded in attracting their attention to general literature in a more effectual manner than any of my predecessors.

My readers will have been accustomed, perhaps, to regard convicts as very ignorant men, but it must be borne in mind that they belong to all classes of society, and if I were to speak of them in the mass, I should say that they were much more intelligent and as well educated as the ordinary peasantry of England. When I commenced reading in prison there were a good many works in the library, which were afterwards withdrawn as being too amusing for the place. These were such works as "The Last Days of Pompeii," "Now and Then," "Adam Bede," "Poor Jack," "Margaret Catchpole," "Irving's Sketch-book," "Dickens's Christmas Tales," &c. There still remained periodicals with tales in them, and these with a mixture of historical, biographical and other-works, constituted the general reading in the work-rooms. The periodicals I note in the order of their popularity, "Chambers's Journal," "Leisure Hour," "Good Words," "The Quiver," "Sunday Magazine," and "Sunday at Home." The reading of an article in the "Leisure Hour," entitled the "Thief in the Confessional," was the chief cause of the readings being discontinued both in the work-rooms and the hospital. As this happened recently and the particulars are still fresh in my memory I will narrate

them here. There were readings aloud in four
hospital and three work-rooms in the prison. In
the hospital the Roman Catholics were kept by
themselves, and had a Roman Catholic reader. In
the prison they were scattered among the Protestants, and in the three work-rooms referred to,
perhaps about one-fifth of the prisoners were
Roman Catholics. In these rooms a Protestant
reader was appointed, and there was no disturbance
about this arrangement until the arrival of a few
Fenians, and a zealous or rather an officious priest.

Shortly after their arrival the other Roman
Catholic prisoners became for the most part Fenians,
and religious animosities soon sprang up among the
prisoners. Macaulay's History of England was
being read by one of my fellow prisoners, in one of
the work-rooms, or sheds, as they were called, when
one of the ignorant and bigoted members of the
Roman Catholic creed got up and objected to its
being read, and complained to the governor on the
subject. The governor, anxious perhaps to please
the new visiting director, who was reported to be a
Roman Catholic, took the complainant's part. The
reading of the book was discontinued, to the great
exultation of the Roman Catholics : however, I got
the same book, and it was read from beginning to end
in the work-room where I was employed ! the
chaplain and the more intelligent Roman Catholics

considering it a very suitable book for the purpose. About this time I wished to be exempted from reading on account of my health, and when I could get a substitute I did give it up for some time; but the substitutes available were not popular with the prisoners, and it was very difficult to find suitable readers amongst them. Two of the Roman Catholics wanted to read, one was a Fenian and a literary man, the other was an ignorant conceited professional thief and an avowed infidel, but they were not allowed : meanwhile the article I have referred to as appearing in the "Leisure Hour," was read in one of the sheds, and it so offended some of the Roman Catholics and the professional thief and infidel who was not allowed to read, that he took the matter before the director, who ordered all reading aloud to be discontinued throughout the prison !

This decision illustrates the usual method adopted by convict authorities in dealing with questions connected with the treatment of prisoners. If a privilege is granted to the convicts and one out of 600 abuses that privilege the 599 will be deprived of it. It was no matter whether the privilege had a good or bad effect upon the majority of the prisoners, if it gave the governor and the directors any trouble they soon put an end to it. If it was a good thing for the prisoners and tended in any way towards the diminution of crime, to have these readings, the directors could have separated the Roman Catholics from the Protestants without any difficulty. If it was a bad thing why was it continued so long? The Roman Catholics had one legitimate ground of complaint, however, in the chaplain having frequently ordered articles to be cut out of "Chambers's Journal," "Good Words," &c. The prisoners naturally asked "Why cut out anything? why not let us judge for ourselves? If the books are good let us have them whole; if bad, reject them altogether; or if there is to be cutting out, why not cut out 'The Thief out of the Confessional,' which is so offensive to the true Catholic?" I happened to read several of the articles which were so cut out, and in several cases one number of a periodical got bound up and in circulation with the condemned article in it. I here note a few articles which were placed in the chaplain's *Index Expurgatorium*, 1st — "Evasions of the Law," an article which appeared in "Good Words," and I may remark that convicts could scarcely be made worse by reading it, for they knew all it contained and probably more than the writer of it did. 2nd—A review of a work by a female warder, in "Chambers's Journal." 3rd— The last half of "The Franklins," a story in the "Leisure Hour." 4th—An article on the "Prisoners' Aid Society" which appeared in the "Quiver," some years ago.

I

In addition to my employments of knitting and reading, I had to go to school one half-day every week for about twelve months, or until a certain class were exempted from attending. On entering the school the prisoner sat until the roll was called, and after half-an-hour was thus spent, he read a couple of verses from the Old Testament, and then listened to an explanation of the passage read. This done, he wrote a short time in his copy book, if he felt inclined, and the proceedings were wound up by a short lecture on some scientific subject. I fear there is not much good done in our convict schools. Teaching, or trying to teach, men ranging from thirty to eighty years of age, who are determined not to learn, or at least so careless about the matter that they never can learn, seems to me a waste of public money. Young men sometimes learn a good deal of French, arithmetic, &c., in prison, but it is not at the school, but from their fellow prisoners that they receive such instruction.

My Sunday routine differed from that of the other days of the week, chiefly in having chapel-going substituted for work, and being allowed to lie in bed an hour longer in the morning.

Shortly after taking up my abode in the twenty-four-bedded room, the diet was changed, and this was the cause of much noise among the convicts. The day fixed for the alteration was a Sunday. The former Sunday's dinner consisted of soup, mutton, and potatoes. The new Sunday dinner was dry bread and four ounces of bad cheese. On being served with this, the prisoners began cursing and swearing, and calling the head officials all the bad names they could think of: "This is what they call Christianity, is it, the ———— hypocrites? Starving a man on Sundays above all days, and then taking us up to that chapel to tell us about mercy and forgiveness and loving our neighbours! This is the way to reform us and make us better, is it ?—By jingo! I will make somebody pay for all this yet. I'll not get my next bit for nothing," &c., &c. Such was the burden of the conversation on this and succeeding Sunday afternoons. To force men to go to hear the Word of God preached when their hearts are full of evil thoughts and their mouths full of curses is far from being a likely mode of leading men to Christ. The chaplain's position in the pulpit used to strike me as being something like that of a farmer sowing good seed broad-cast over a field so overgrown with tares, that the seed could never reach the soil. If he attempts to clear the soil of the weeds, to win the hearts of the prisoners, he finds the whole system of prison discipline arrayed against him. That discipline breeds and encourages the growth of every evil passion in the heart of man, and he, the chaplain, is part of that system : he lives by it, and he is not allowed to interfere with it, at all events he never did so. When prisoners complained to him of some injustice or some cruelty, they got for reply : "I am here to preach the Gospel, and I can do nothing in the matter."

Chaplains paid by the State, and forming part of the penal establishment, can never do much good to the prisoners, except in so far as they operate as a check upon the cruelty or neglect of the governor and other officers. Missionaries having no connection with Government, might do some good amongst them. At the time I commenced to attend the prison chapel, I learned that a score or so of convicts took the sacrament. Some of them were truly pious, as far as one could judge in such matters, others were unfit or unworthy partakers, the whole of them were called by the other prisoners "Parson's men," or "Sacrament blokes," and it used to pain me to hear them scoffed and mocked at. It was a great victory if they could be got to swear on the evening of the communion day : I never could make up my mind to become a "Parson's man," for reasons perhaps not very satisfactory, even to myself. In the first place I belonged to another branch of the church; then I had only one leg and could not kneel at the altar, and would have felt while standing something like a beggar in dirty rags in a fine pew among silks and satins; then again I would have lost my influence over many of my fellow-prisoners. I may have been wrong in all this, but as I once said to my fellow-prisoners when appealed to on the subject of religion, "There are only three cardinal points in my religious belief, and these are simple and easily remembered—believe in Christ, love God, and love my neighbour; what I do inconsistent with the last I know to be wrong. It is inconsistent, I think, with the latter, for Protestants to revile and speak evil of Roman Catholics, and *vice versâ*, therefore I disapprove of discussions and arguments on religious belief among prisoners, as they usually lead to feelings incompatible with true neighbourly love." Such was my reply to a question addressed to me by a convict during a hot debate between the Protestants and Roman Catholics, and it allayed the storm instantly. As a rule I avoided and discountenanced all discussion on theological subjects.

After I had been four weeks in the prison I began to get a little downhearted at finding myself so far removed from sympathy. In the hospital I had an occasional chat with a Scripture-reader, but here there was no one with whom I could have any intellectual conversation, and no visitors were allowed. I felt very sad and dispirited for a time, and wrote to my friends that I should like to have a visit from a clergyman of my own persuasion who resided in London. I got for a reply a visit from some of my own friends, who mentioned that the gentleman whose visit I desired was too much occupied with his own flock to look after a lost sheep like me. I notice this chiefly in order to remark that this was a kind of turning point in my prison career: the point at which the generality of prisoners turn from bad to worse, and when long imprisonment ceases to be an instrument for good; when human sympathy is sought, and by the great majority of prisoners sought in vain, and when in consequence they seek to obtain the sympathy of their evil companions, and begin in earnest that downward career which knows no shame, and finds its goal in the convict's grave.

CHAPTER XI

A S I have already said in a previous chapter,
one of the most glaring defects in our present
system of penal servitude, viewed as a means of reformation as well as of punishment, is the indiscriminate association of all classes of criminals, or rather
all criminals with a certain sentence, irrespective of
the nature of the crime they have committed, the
previous character of the criminal or the probability of his re-admission into society as an honest
and useful member of it. I have met in the
same ward prisoners of widely different characters and
antecedents, whose crimes afforded conclusive proofs
that in habits, disposition, and general conduct, they
would never, in the natural order of things, become
associates, compelled by law to mate with each other
as equals, and to learn of each other how to injure,
not how to benefit society and themselves. There
are, for instance, certain crimes which a man may
commit under the influence of strong passions, aroused
in moments of great temptation, such as rape ; or of

great provocation, such as manslaughter; or committed under the pressure of misfortune, or to avoid
impending ruin, such as forgery or embezzlement,
which do not necessarily prove the criminal to be
of habitually depraved habits, or generally of a violent and vicious disposition. I found as a rule
prisoners guilty of these crimes undergoing their
first sentences. Prison life and prison associations
were new to them as to me. They had no inclination to repeat the offence, or to pursue a career
of crime, but rather disposed to redeem their character,
and live an honest and industrious life. Yet this
class of prisoners are condemned, in addition to the
loss of liberty and character, to live in constant
contact, for years it may be, with the professional
thief and house-breaker, the burglar, and the
garotter, who has been frequently convicted, and
whose whole life is spent between the prison and
the " cross." The natural and inevitable result of
this is contamination. Even in the case of men
possessing high principle and of great moral forti-
tude the effect would be deteriorating and pernicious.
With men of weak resolution, strong passions, and a
comparatively low standard of morality, the consequences cannot be doubtful in the majority of cases.
They gradually lose self-respect, cease to think of
reformation or amendment, in time they come to
envy the hardened stoicism and "gameness" of the
practised ruffian, learn his language, imbibe his no-

tions of life, and finally resolve, since character, self-respect, and all else that bind them to morality and virtue are lost, that they will compel society to make amends for the ruin it has brought upon them. It is from this class I am persuaded that the ranks of our born and bred convicts are so largely and so constantly supplemented. Yet how easily and how speedily might this source of supply be diminished, if not altogether closed.

The old Transportation Act, although it may not have provided for any such separation as that I have just indicated, and although it was based on what I consider pernicious principles, was undoubtedly the most effectual plan for getting rid of our criminal population, and in its operation the most merciful to the prisoner of any of our recent parliamentary enactments. Had its provisions been efficiently and judiciously administered, we might still have been sending convicts to our colonies. But the business of exporting our " dirty linen " was grossly mismanaged. The merchant who hopes to succeed as an exporter must study carefully the class of goods suitable for the market he proposes to supply, and send only those he is confident will be approved of and meet a ready sale. But our prison authorities, by some fatality, so organized the system of selection of convicts for transportation that those who were, of all men, the very last a young and virtuous community would seek, were forced upon them, whilst those for whom there was a constant demand, and who would have regarded transportation and liberation abroad as the opportunity for escaping from social prejudice, of retrieving their lost character, and of commencing anew a life of honesty and industry, were condemned to pine in the prisons at home, and in too many cases, to adopt a career of crime when their sentences expired. The first and great commandment the prison authorities regarded in their selection was, that the prisoner should be physically healthy, sound in wind and limb; and the second was, that he should have been a certain time in prison at home after receiving his last sentence and conducted himself well whilst there. No enquiry was made into the prisoner's previous history, employment, education, or general disposition and habits, which, one would naturally have thought necessary before any intelligent opinion could be formed as to the probabilities of his future career abroad. Now, although the qualifications of health and good conduct might seem to be good and sufficient grounds on which to make such a selection as was required for transportation, those acquainted with prisoners and prison life will at once perceive that they were very far from being so. In the first place, a great many of the prisoners who would have adopted an honest life and been a benefit to the colonies if they had been sent there, but who were rejected on account of ill-health, had become diseased in prison and in consequence of their imprisonment, and would in all probability have recovered their usual good health before they had reached their destination abroad. These were generally men of education, and accustomed to generous diet, but the prison discipline and scale of dietary soon told upon their health, and disqualified them in the eyes of the prison officials for the boon of transportation. Even if their health was not restored by the sea voyage and liberation abroad, it was only exchanging the hospital abroad for the hospital at home. If the experiment succeeded, who may estimate its value to him who was the subject of it? Again, "good conduct," as indicated by the standard of our prison authorities, is anything but a trustworthy criterion of the convict's true character and disposition. It does not mean that the prisoner has shown himself honest, industrious, or well disposed, or in any active sense what the phrase is ordinarily supposed to mean; indeed the system of penal servitude does not permit the prisoner any opportunity of showing that he is so. All that "good conduct," in prison official language means is, that the prisoner has not broken any of the prison rules, and is therefore a purely negative quality; scrupulous obedience to prison discipline and regulations, with severe penalties attached to transgression, is a very

sorry basis on which to found a character of good
conduct in a convict. The consequence was, if one
of the greatest ruffians that ever entered the prison
gates were to make up his mind, as I have known
many of them do, to go abroad, he knew that he had
only to study the rules of the prison and obey them
for a certain length of time, and he would obtain
his object, and be let loose among the innocent
colonists, to rob and murder as he found opportunity.
Thousands of such men, who had purposely be-
haved themselves well in the prison at home, with
the grim determination of making amends for their
restraint by a career of increased violence and
ruffianism abroad, were thus let loose upon colonial
society, and there is no wonder that the colonies
rose up in indignation and shut their ports against
them.   As a rule, it was the hardened criminal
whose reformation under existing laws was, I may
safely say, entirely out of the question, who, on the
score of health and good conduct, most perfectly
fulfilled the conditions required by the prison
authorities, and most frequently had the boon of
transportation extended to him.   Accustomed by
long and frequent experience to prison diet and discipline, and to all the "dodges" for augmenting the
one and evading or modifying the other, he could
keep himself in perfect health under circumstances
which would send a less experienced and more

sensitive man to the hospital in a month; whilst his familiarity with all the petty rules and regulations of the prison, which the novice is in constant danger of breaking (quite unintentionally), enabled him to steer clear of any offence that could be reported if he thought it for his interest to strive for the convict's prize. In fact, "good conduct," as exemplified by a convict according to the prison standard, affords no more reliable evidence of his moral qualities and industrious habits, than proficiency in drill affords of the moral character of the private soldier.

It is quite clear that selection on these terms could only by a rare accident find the suitable men for sending abroad. And yet it is my firm conviction that I, or any other man possessing ordinary intelligence and insight into human character and experience of convict life, could, with the utmost ease, have selected from the inmates of our prisons a very large number for exportation, whom our colonists would have been glad to receive, and who would have been rescued from a life of ignominy or crime at home. The question may very naturally be asked— Why could not our prison officials have done the same? The only answer I can give is that our prison officials (excepting, the very highest) are directly interested in *maintaining* and *increasing*, and not in *re- ducing*, the number of our convicts, and they are therefore inclined to favour the liberation of those whom they are pretty sure will soon return. -

As a fair and forcible example of the advantage which might have been taken of the "Transportation Act," in dealing with a certain class of prisoners, and also as an illustration—not nearly so forcible as others I have alluded to, and will yet notice—of the fault of the authorities in the matter of selection, I will mention one case. Three young men received sentence of twenty years' penal servitude for rape. One of them, quite a youth, was more a spectator of than a principal in the crime, the other two being the really guilty parties. The three were in due course sent to Portsmouth. The guilty pair were sent abroad, and liberated before the end of five years from the date of their conviction. One of them is now married and settled comfortably abroad, and the other lodges with him. The other prisoner, being young and not very muscular, received some injury while at work and was sent to the Invalid Criminal Hospital in Surrey, and has to remain in prison, in a state useless to himself and to society, for eight or nine years longer than his more guilty companions.

But the day has gone by for successful re-establishment of a penal colony. I do not think there are many who would commit crimes for the express purpose of getting abroad, unless the colony was very attractive; but no country where officers can be got to reside will ever be looked upon with dread by the majority of criminals. A penal colony, I am convinced, would have no deterring influence on the minds of those convicts who are most difficult to deal with. It would have such an effect upon certain classes of prisoners, but their numbers are small, and less expensive remedies might be found even more effectual in their cases.

When convicts leave prison they could be divided into three classes. First, those men who are not only determined to live honestly, but who in all human probability will never again enter a prison; their number may amount to about ten per cent. of the whole. Another class leave prison with the deliberate intention of committing crime, and their number may be about forty per cent. The third class, comprising about fifty per cent. of the whole, belong to the hesitating, unsteady, wavering class. Many of this class do manage to keep out of prison, but at least one half of them return, and, along with the forty per cent. of professionals, bring up the number of the re-convicted to seventy per cent. Now, it must be quite clear that if we would reduce this number, it is to the fifty per cent. of waverers that our efforts must be principally directed. The other classes either do not require or will not benefit by our endeavours. Our present law is altogether unable to cure the professional thief. I never heard, and I never met with a convict who ever heard, of any of this class being converted into honest men by the operation of our present system, nor do I believe it possible to point to a single case. The professional thief lacks three virtues—economy, industry, honesty. Now, under the present system it is positively forbidden to give him any practical lesson either in economy or honesty; industry, indeed, might be taught him, but he rarely if ever receives an intelligent lesson, for it must be remembered that enforced labour does not teach the labourer industry, but is more likely to inspire him with an aversion to it. All that can be done with the professional thief, under existing laws, beyond the punishment of confinement and vigorous prison discipline, possibly, is to give him such work to do as he can do, or be readily taught to do, and that work not to be of the kind usually done in prison, but such as will compensate to some extent for his maintenance in prison, and enable him to live honestly out of it should he so elect.

On my right hand, in the twenty-four-bedded room, lay a city-bred professional thief, acquainted with all the brothels and sinks of iniquity in London, and his disgusting conversation chiefly related to such places. Like many of his class, his constitution was delicate, and his appetite somewhat dainty. The prison fare and hard work were undoubtedly severe punishment to him; but no punishment could frighten him into honesty. He knew no honest trade by which he could support himself, but if he had been taught one in prison such as suited his strength and talents, and had been taught only the *policy* of honesty, and been then sent to a country far removed from his old haunts, where his newly-organized trade would be more profitable than thieving, the possibility is he would have become a useful man in the world. On the expiration of his sentence, which was three years, he went home and wrote back to one of his "pals" in prison, under an assumed name, that he had been to the Prisoners' Aid Society, and had obtained as much of his gratuity as he could, to buy a barrow and some fruit, as he meant to turn costermonger. He added, however, that he did not like fruit-selling, and returned to his old trade of "gunsmith," gunning being the slang term for thieving, or going on the cross. The real fact was, that he never intended anything else than being a "gunsmith," but only used the deception in order to obtain a little more money from the Aid Society than he otherwise could. As soon as he got his barrow and stock he sold all off, and in a very few months I had him for a companion again, with a seven years' sentence. I remember asking whether he preferred a sentence of seven years' penal servitude, or three years in Coldbath Fields?"

K

"Three years in Coldbath Fields ! why that would kill me.   I would as soon have fifteen years here ."

The only good trait discoverable in his character was his ardent affectiou for his mother.   When he has completed about five years and three months he will be liberated again, if he is alive, and again he will return to crime; and it is almost impossible that such a man can do otherwise; and as long as our prison authorities regard convicts as mere living automatons, all modelled after the same fashion in iniquity, our convict and county prisons, viewed as reformatories, will remain quite inoperative for good, but very potent for evil.

CHAPTER XII.

HOW REBELS AGAINST SOCIETY ARE MADE—I AM REMOVED TO A SMALL
ROOM AMONGST MURDERERS—THE "HIGHFLYER" AGAIN—HOW A
YOUNG GENTLEMAN WAS MADE A WARNING TO OTHERS.

A CERTAIN class of criminals—it would be very
wrong to say all—may be looked upon as rebels
against society, and assuming that they are so, it
would be difficult to conceive a more effective method
of promoting and disseminating the spirit of rebellion than that which is adopted in our convict establishments. We collect all these rebels from the
various counties into a few localities, 600 here, 1000
there, and 1500 somewhere else, and along with
them we place a certain proportion of comparatively
untainted men. We subject them to a course of
rigorous discipline in matters of diet and exercise,
the sole effect of which is to stimulate them still
more against society. We allow them a certain
amount of intercourse with each other; liberty to
the old to contaminate the young; to the veteran
ruffian to enlist and drill the new recruit; to all
to plan their new campaigns, and hatch new con-

K 2

spiracies, and then disperse them throughout the country to sow the seeds of sedition, and raise the standard of rebellion wherever they may go. This is really what is being done in our convict prisons. Take an extreme case, and keep out of sight altogether the characters and dispositions of our criminals, and imagine a hundred of England's most steady, honest, and industrious working men placed in our convict establishments for a few years, and what would be the result? It would most probably be this: if they were young, and had only received an imperfect education, fifty of them would join some branch of the thief professsion if kept by force in convict society for three years; seventy of them would do so if kept for six years; and if kept ten years, they would almost all be corrupted, and become when liberated a source of corruption themselves.

But if the hardened and incorrigible criminals were really punished in any proportion to the others the system would have a kind of consistent iniquity about it which it does not possess. My left-hand companion was an old agricultural labourer, one of a large class to whom a convict prison is no punishment. He had been brought up to work, and although an old man, he could work far more than a city thief, and yet not work hard. He had brought up a family who were all scattered abroad. He had now no real home when out of prison, and his third penal sentence of fourteen years was very much lighter punishment to him than fourteen days, with loss of character, would be to anyone in the upper or middle classes of society. I met many such men in prison, and I used to ask them how much money they would take to do my sentence in addition to their own? One would say 100*l.*, another, 50*l.*, another 40*l.*, and some would even take considerably less.

Imprisonment with hard labour will never have the slightest effect in deterring such men from committing crime. Labour that would soon kill many other men would not punish them, but they would prefer it even to sitting in school. Rough fare they can do with, as long as it fills the belly. They have no other ambition to gratify. With the stomach distended and a quid of tobacco in their mouths, they are as happy as kings, and very careless about liberty. Many of them when they leave the prison, leave home. To such men, and to all the class of vagrant and pauper criminals, a convict prison means a comfortable home, where they are fed and clothed, and bathed and physicked, and have all their wants supplied, without trouble or care, in exchange for their liberty and such labour as they can easily and cheaply perform. To the professional thieves a convict prison is a Court of Bankruptcy, to be avoided if possible, and to be made the most of when unavoidable. A place of punishment no doubt, but punishment nearly useless and entirely misdirected. To the man who has wrought for his living at some honest trade, up to the commission of his first known offence, who has been accounted respectable by his neighbours, and who belongs to a class of society with whom loss of character is utter ruin—a convict prison is a Hell. If he happen also to be a man of thought and education, it will in addition appear to be an institution for robbing honest tax-payers, and a nursery of vice and crime, which all good men should endeavour to reform or destroy.

In the small room to which I was now removed, the lodgers were quiet, inoffensive men, and in a few cases apparently religious.

During my residence in the prison I was frequently removed from one room to another, to suit the convenience of the prison authorities. Fortunately I had no rent to pay, no economy to study, no opportunity to practice honesty, and my effects were easily carried about. Obedience—the soldiers' virtue—and civility, were all I had to study, and these were not difficult to practice in my own case. One class of prisoners in these rooms were elderly men, who had committed murder, or manslaughter, and who, from their age and infirmities had missed being sent to Western Australia. I knew upwards of twenty of them, and generally speaking, they were quiet inoffensive men, with no inclination to steal or to do wrong. Several of them had very hot tempers, all of them, indeed, who committed their crimes under the influence of anger; others I sympathized with a good deal, inasmuch as they had been sorely tempted, and seemed penitent and honest.

One of them had brought up a family of honest working men. After the death of their mother, he married and lived with another woman, who was addicted to intemperance, and he was so annoyed at her conduct and by her tongue, that his passion obtained the mastery over him, and in a moment of frenzy he killed her. This prisoner had had his arm broken at Portland, which prevented his being sent abroad, whence he would have been liberated by this time.

Another case was that of a comparatively young man, who shot his sweetheart because she had chosen another man just as the prisoner was looking forward to his marriage with her. He tried to shoot himself at the same time, but the shot passed through the jaw and cheek bones, leaving him in a sadly disfigured condition to meet his doom of penal servitude for life.

I met several cases where murder was committed through jealousy. One man murdered his wife for flirting or cohabiting with another man. A second murdered the paramour and spared his wife, and so on. In the majority of these cases, the prisoners were very unlikely to commit a second offence.

There was one very peculiar case which I will here mention. The prisoner was the worst cripple perhaps in the prison, and the quietest man in it. He rarely spoke to anyone unless he was first spoken to, and his answers were very brief. This man committed a deliberate murder; although he had only one arm and but one good leg. He lay in wait for his victim, and his motive for perpetrating the deed was not money but revenge. The person he killed had injured or defrauded his father before he died, and being unable to obtain justice he took revenge, and is now paying the full penalty. He sits in the workroom along with the others, but being paralyzed he is not compelled to work at anything.

Another peculiar case was that of a man who had starved his mother to death, in order to obtain possession of her money. He was a miser, and was often taunted for his crime by the thief fraternity. He was the filthiest neighbour I ever had. Most of the prisoners are cleanly in their habits, but this one was the reverse. He would have his food stored away beside him, rather than give it to a fellow prisoner. He was not a great eater, and at one time there was more food about than the prisoners could consume; but whatever he got he kept until it was taken from him. After being confined for about thirteen years, he was allowed to go to North America, on a conditional pardon, to a son who lived there. Among the many petitions I drew out for prisoners to copy, his was the only one that ever succeeded. I have written petitions for dying men to the Home Secretary, for permission to go out and die at home, and many without any just grounds at all, but none succeeded, save the one I have mentioned above.

I have repeatedly asked prisoners under sentences of penal servitude for life whether they would prefer that sentence to being hanged. The general reply was " I would rather be 'topt' at once, and be out of my misery, than remain in prison all my days." " It's bad enough when I have the prospect of liberty in twelve years." " If they are going to keep men in prison all their days, and torture them besides, they'll commit suicide or murder in prison. Look at Townley, who threw himself over the stair-railings at Pentonville and killed himself."

Such would be the answers I would receive to my questions on this subject. With reference to Townley's case I was told by an intelligent prisoner, who knew him and saw him commit suicide, that it was committed mainly in consequence of the cruel, absurd and childish system of suppressing a prisoner's letters to his friends, on grounds usually hostile to the interests of society, viz., the concealment of truth.

Another class of prisoners were " coiners." These were generally " fly-men." They knew every point of the law on the subject, and as a rule returned to their profession as soon as they got their " ticket." Prison is no doubt a great punishment to such men, because they can make a good living at their business; but I question if ever there was a reformed coiner. They are usually well-conducted prisoners, that is, they are civil and do what they are told, but their influence over others is very pernicious. A very considerable number of the convicts left the prison with the intention of "hawking" from place to place, and doing a little bit on the " cross" when they saw the coast clear, which meant either stealing or " snyde-pitching." These hawkers found friends in the coiners, who would tell them where they could get the bad money, so that if they could not work themselves they could do a friend a turn in the way of business. I knew several instances of prisoners with a first conviction getting a second in consequence of being told where to get bad money; and I knew many more who will, in all human probability, meet with the same fate from the same cause.

Another of my fellow prisoners was a singular specimen. I have already referred to him as being almost the only " highflyer " in the prison, as being the man who once obtained 150*l.* from a gentleman in Devonshire under false pretences. This man was not ranked among the *"aristocs"* in prison society, although he was in many respects their equal or superior in certain branches of education. And here I may remark that on parade, where all the prisoners exercised together, they associated in classes as they would do outside—the "roughs," the "prigs," the "needy-mizzlers," and the "aristocs," keeping, not always, but pretty much among themselves. There were only a few of the class termed "aristocs." and they comprised men who had been clergymen, merchants, bankers, editors, surgeons, &c. These were usually my associates during the exercise time. Now the "highflyer" I have referred to did not belong to this class, but except in his principles and habits and tastes, his education was quite equal to theirs. He spoke German and French fluently, knew Latin and Greek, a smattering of Italian, and the higher branches of mathematics. What first surprised me about him was his pretended intimacy with some German merchants of the highest standing I knew in London, and with whom I had done business. To know such men I afterwards found was part of his profession. He could tell me not only the names and titles of the nobility and gentry, but the names of their families, where many of them were educated, to whom they were married, and many other particulars of their private history. His sentence was three years, and I believe he got it something in this way. He had been in the country following his profession, and had obtained some money, I think

thirty pounds, from a gentleman of "his acquaintance."
In the country he was the Reverend Dr. So and So,
with a white neck-tie and all the surroundings of a
clergyman. In London he was a "swell," with a
cigar in his mouth.

It so happened that the benevolent gentleman
from whom he had obtained the money came to
town and recognized the "Doctor," when cutting the
swell, and had him apprehended and punished. He
had been several times in county prisons, but, as he
always changed his name and his localities, this fact
was not known officially. He was an avowed infidel,
and seemed to delight in spreading his opinions
among the prisoners, who were generally too willing
to listen to him. If he keeps out of prison, it will
be his cleverness in escaping detection and not his
principles that will save him. His prison influence
was most pernicious, and afforded another striking
and painful illustration of the evils of indiscriminate
association of prisoners. I maintain that it formed
no part of any prisoner's sentence that, in addition
to all the other horrors of penal servitude, he should
be placed within the sphere of this man's influence
and such as he; and the system which not only
permits but demands that his moral and religious
interests should be thus imperilled, if not altogether
corrupted and destroyed, undertakes a fearful responsibility.

The next case I will notice will illustrate the truth of what I have advanced on this point. It was that of a young man, P——, who had been respectably educated, and whose crime was simply the foolish frolic of a giddy youth. He had engaged a dog-cart to drive to London, a distance somewhere about fifty miles from where he resided. He had another youth for his companion, and they both got on the "spree" in London. Some shark picked them up, and bought the horse and dog-cart from them at a merely nominal price. When they got sober they returned home, and this youth went and told the proprietor of the dog-cart what he had done, and (according to his own statement) offered, through his friends, to pay for it. The proprietor was so enraged, however, that nothing but the prosecution of the prisoner would satisfy him, and he was sentenced to ten years' penal servitude. He had the character of a "fast" youth, and met with a severe judge. This prisoner might have been easily led into the path of honour and usefulness, if the attempt had been honestly made. Whoever his judge was, if he were an Englishman and father of a family, he would never again pass sentence of penal servitude on such a youth for any offence against property, if he knew as well as I do what the sentence involves. Shut up any such man for seven years in a place where the only men of his own age are city-bred thieves, and what can be ex-

pected of him? This young man elected the smartest
and cleverest of the London pickpockets for his companions. They made a tool of him in prison, and
unless his friends have managed to get him sent
abroad, he is very likely acting as a "stall" for some
of his old companions now. He never learnt anything in prison except *knitting*. He was also one
of the "readers," but most of his time was spent in
hospital. He could spit blood when he chose, and
the doctor being more liberal to him than many
others, for several very natural reasons, the prisoner
used this liberality to benefit some of his "pals" who
could not manage to get the good things they wanted
from the doctor otherwise. In return for this kindness he would get an inch or two of tobacco, or
"snout," as it was usually termed. When other
means failed to procure this luxury, he would write
to his friends for a toothbrush and sell it for the
weed, which caused the toothbrushes to be withdrawn from all the prisoners. Then he would write
for a pair of spectacles, pretending that his eyes were
getting weak. These he sold, and the last were discovered passing into one of the cooks' hands in fair
exchange for mutton chops. They were taken into
the governor's room, and after being examined by
that potentate they were laid on his desk, and next
morning they were nowhere to be found; they were
stolen, but *not* by a prisoner. Of course, P——

knew nothing about his spectacles, when examined on the subject, except that some one must have taken them from his shelf. The result was that all spectacles belonging to the prisoners were called in, and prison "glasses" issued in their stead. The spectacles were intended ultimately to reach the hands of an officer for tobacco, and if they had not been removed from the desk, the officer might have got his discharge and the prisoner a severe punishment. This was one of the thousand - and - one schemes which prisoners resort to in order to get "snout," and without the aid of an officer they can get none.

This youth was intended by his parents for the church, but was trained in prison to be a thief, as "a warning to others"—and his was far from being a solitary case.

CHAPTER XIII.

THE ACT OF 1864—CLASSIFICATION OF PRISONERS—THE MARK SYSTEM :
ITS DEFECTS—THE TRUE CRIMINAL LAW OF RESTITUTION—THE ONLY
METHOD BY WHICH CONFIRMED CRIMINALS MAY BE RECLAIMED—
WORKHOUSES.

THE year 1864 was a marked epoch in convict life. A new Act was then passed and fresh prison [regulations were brought into force. This Act contained one good clause, viz., the abolition of three and four years' sentences. In one year as many as 1800 men were sentenced to three and four years' penal servitude, being a large proportion of the total number. Such men are now for the most part sentenced to eighteen months and two years' imprisonment, which will account for a decrease in the number of convicts and an increase in the number of county prisoners. This is a short step in the right direction. The convict directors take credit to themselves for this reduction in the number of convicts, and boast that they have at last found the true panacea for criminal diseases. A report to that effect, cut out of a newspaper, was circulated amongst the prisoners, and their indignation was great at the way in which the public were "gulled" about themselves and prison treatment. No doubt a few more thieves and burglars are driven to pursue their callings in France and America by the operation of the new police regulations, and I freely admit that a few more may annually be sent into another world by the same means, but no one can yet point to a reformed professional "Cracksman," "Coiner," "Hoister," or "Screwsman," as proof of the beneficial results of the change. The most unpopular clause in the Act was that relating to police surveillance. The majority of the prisoners were very much annoyed at this regulation, some of them, indeed, would much rather have remained in prison than encounter it. For my own part, I approve of the principle of surveillance. I see in it the germ of a system whereby a large class of criminals may ultimately be punished entirely outside the prison walls. I object, however, to the police being entrusted with the duty. Their proper business is to catch the thief and preserve order. The surveillance of liberated prisoners ought to be entrused to those who are directly interested in empty jails, and who would endeavour to assist the liberated men either in getting employment or to emigrate.

With reference to the *classification* of prisoners which commenced under the Act of 1864, I have no hesitation in saying that it is a gross fraud upon the

L

public, a delusion and a snare. The error which I pointed out in a former chapter, as being committed in the selection of convicts for transportation, is here repeated and in a more aggravated form, if that were possible. By the new Act the prisoners were divided into four great classes. Into the fourth, or "probation class," all prisoners were required to enter on being admitted into prison. After a certain time, if the prisoner was so fortunate as to escape being "reported" for any offence against the prison rules, he would be placed in the third class, and again, after being a certain time in the third class he was passed, subject to the same condition, into the second, and so on. Should he have made any mistake and allowed himself to get "reported," he either missed his chance of getting into the higher, or was degraded into a lower class. The object of this classification no doubt was to get all the well-behaved men together, but the blunder committed was in making obedience to the prison rules the only test of qualification for the higher classes. This, as I have already explained, was really worse than no test at all, because the frequently convicted criminal, who was thoroughly posted up in all points of prison discipline and regulations, was more likely than the novice to escape being "reported" for violation of them. The consequence is, that in respect of character, disposition and moral quality, there is really no difference to be found amongst the men in any of the classes. The scheme operates in this way—suppose that a clergyman by some mischance gets sentenced to penal servitude, and enters the prison in company with one of the very worst villains that could be selected out of our criminal population; both these men, the one with a first sentence, the other with a long string of convictions against him, enter the "probation class" at Millbank, on precisely the same terms. The "jail bird," knowing all about the ways of the prison, would probably pass with ease into the third class. The clergyman, being new to the discipline, might make a mistake and get "reported," and in that way would not be so likely to reach the third class so soon as the other; but granting that he did so they would still be together, the man inured to guilt and crime would still be beside the new and casual lodger, the man who had never been in prison before would still have the opportunity of learning the evil ways of the confirmed rogue. Again, should the clergyman be fortunate enough in passing into the higher classes at the usual time, the jail bird would certainly not be behind.

If a thousand prisoners, from all parts of the country, of all ages, habits, and antecedents, were brought to one of our convict establishments, they would go through their time in the same way, good, bad, and indifferent, all together. The clergyman, even if he were to get into prison innocently, and were the best Christian in the world, would never get rid of the jail-bird; and in the highest class his companions would be no better than those in the lowest.

I grant that our directors could not classify convicts according to their real merits, any more than a quack doctor could classify patients suffering from disease; but although they cannot have the knowledge necessary to do it properly, they might do a little in the right direction. The quack, even, would know cholic from consumption, diarrhœa from dropsy; so any man of sense would be able to distinguish between a case of chronic moral disease and a case of partial or temporary paralysis of the moral faculty!

The system of "marks," as it is called in prison, is the most prominent feature in the new regulations, and is based upon the same absurd principle as the classification clause. The rule relating to marks specifies "That the time which every convict under sentence of penal servitude must henceforth pass in prison will be regulated by a certain number of marks, which he must earn by actual labour performed before he can be discharged."

The method adopted is to debit the prisoner with a certain number of marks, according to the length of his sentence, and if he performs the whole of the work required of him he is credited with as many marks as would represent a fourth part of his sentence.

If this law were carried out in its integrity it would be most cruel and unjust. Fortunately for the prisoners it is not very strictly adhered to—at least not at the prison where I was confined—the officers making allowance for the prisoners' infirmities. To show how it would operate, let us take the case of the clergyman and the jail-bird once more. Assuming that the former was a stout and healthy man, and able to work, but not having been accustomed to it, really not able to do much of it, and that the latter had been at the work for years—which would win in the race for liberty, if the law was strictly enforced? The probability is that the clergyman would not earn a single day's remission, whilst the jail-bird would get one-fourth of his time remitted; and assuming that both had the same sentence originally, would go a considerable way into a "fresh bit" before the poor clergyman had finished his first sentence.

The "mark" system admits of great cruelty being practised, but on the whole, as it is carried out, it is a more innocent piece of deception than the classification. At the public works, however, there is much injustice done by it, no allowance being made for a sick man, unless he has met with some accident. If the "marks" were money, *bonâ fide* sovereigns, and if the prisoner were permitted to exercise the abilities God has given him in order to earn that money, there might be some sense and justice discernable in the system. As it is there is neither.

I may here venture to say that we might materially diminish crime and expense connected with the prosecution and punishment of criminals by doing away with our convict establishments altogether, except for the confinement of political prisoners, and those having sentences for life. In lieu of these I would suggest the introduction of the system of remissions into our county jails, granting first offenders a liberal, and third and fourth, an extremely small allowance. Teaching the prisoners such trades as they are fitted for, qualifying them for colonists, and selecting the most suitable for emigration. I would also place the jails and workhouses under one management. Commissioners for the prevention of crime and pauperism in each county, and subject them to a rigid government inspection by a board responsible to Parliament and the nation.

But even this would only be a partial reform. I would have our criminal laws based upon the old Mosaic principle of "enforced restitution," and carried out on the Christian principle of making the offender "pay the uttermost farthing." Then we could fairly and justly retain the idle and the useless in the net of justice, and allow the willing and industrious to achieve their own freedom by satisfying the claims of the law.

Now, when time has been strangled, and virtue repressed, we allow the worst villains to escape, and all that has been required of them in prison was civility to officers, obedience to a stupid discipline, and a few years' work which neither enables them to support an honest livelihood outside the prison, or contributes in any appreciable degree to their maintenance inside.

Under the system I propose, every man who stole a sheep would have to pay the same penalty before he could exercise the rights of citizenship—no matter whether his character was good, bad, or indifferent; no matter whether he was rich or poor, a peer or a peasant, the voice of impartial justice would say, " You have incurred the same debt to the State, and the same penalty must be paid."

At present every man who steals a sheep has to pay a different penalty. This man is sentenced to six months, that other to twelve months, and then another to fifteen years of penal servitude, according to the discretion of the judge; and instead of being made to pay the price of the sheep and the costs of his prosecution, he becomes a grievous burden to the honest tax-payer, who has to supply him with chaplains, schoolmasters, surgeons, cooks, bakers, tailors, and a whole host of servants in livery to minister to his wants, and so unfit him for the practice of economy, frugality, and other kindred virtues when his fetters are cut. Under a law based on the principle of restitution, the man of good character and industrious habits might be able to find sureties to enable him to discharge his debt to the State under the surveillance of the authorities, 'without being surrounded by prison walls. The man of middling character might only have a limited amount of liberty, such as the responsible authorities might grant him. Whilst the man of bad character would have to discharge his debt inside prison walls, where he might still continue a villain in habits and heart, and increase his debt by fresh acts of dishonesty; but this would be his own fault, and the safety-valve of the machinery.

But to return to the Act 1864. If the labour performed under the "mark" system was either remunerative, or such as a convict might obtain an honest living at when liberated, the system could not be condemned as utterly bad. But if we except the tailoring and the shoemaking done for the use of the establishment, there are really no other employments suitable for the general class of men who find their way into prison. The professional thief—and I am now speaking of the *reformation* as well as the punishment of criminals—requires to be taught some trade for which he has a natural aptitude before it is possible for him to gain a livelihood, and he must be taught it well, for unless he is a skilled workman he

would not be worth the wages necessary to keep him
out of temptation. To go on punishing such men in
the hope that we will make them honest, is absurd; and
to persevere in "reforming," them without teaching
them practically that which is indispensable to their
remaining honest, is equally ridiculous. We may
train a boy to be a labourer of almost any sort, and
can impart moral and religious instruction to an
unformed mind with success, but if we attempt to do
either of them with a confirmed thief who has not
been taught to work, we must be disappointed in the
result. The *first* step to reformation, is to interest
him in some employment suitable to his abilities,
and any other step taken before this only hinders or
prevents the work of reformation. We have never
yet taken this first step, consequently we have never
yet succeeded in reforming any of them. It is also
essential that such work should be also well paid,
and that the money made at such employment should
be his passport to liberty. Under the present system
we only make him kill time at labour which disgusts
him with all kinds of regular industry. The county
prison sentences are, moreover, too short to enable
the thief to earn such a passport to freedom, but
they are of just the requisite length and fitness for
turning the casual into the confirmed criminal. In
fact, *time* sentences are not suitable for confirmed
thieves. Their sentences ought to be so much money

to be earned in a penal workshop, where honesty and economy could be practised as well as industry. There are two grave objections urged against teaching thieves lucrative trades. Firstly,—it would tempt others to commit crime; and secondly, it would interfere with free labour. With regard to the first objection, I admit there would be some force in it if the sentences were such as they are now, because time runs on, whether the prisoner is industrious or not. But if the sentence imposed a fine in addition to all the expenses incurred by the prisoner during his incarceration, there would then be no inducement to the commission of crime. With reference to the second objection, I would merely state that all labour done in prison of a useful character interferes with free labour to some extent, but I contend that if each prisoner was employed at that kind of work for which he is best qualified, it would interfere less with the proper and necessary division of free labour than the present plan of keeping a large number of men employed at work for which they have no special aptitude.

The error we have made in employing prisoners hitherto is not merely that we have employed them at trades or other employments not suitable to their natural abilities, but that we have entered into competition with those trades where too much competition already exists. We should never have allowed

smart young pickpockets to compete with poor semp-
stresses, whose ranks are already overcrowded. There
will always be plenty of honest people descending in
the social scale to do underpaid work, and there are
thousands of petty thieves who are not fit for any
other. So that there is a greater need for elevating
the clever professional thief to the position of a skilled
artisan.

The city bred thief class are far from being dunces
or "flats," and it is not possible to make them
common labourers. Many of them may very fitly
be compared to the idle and dissipated "swells" of
the middle and higher classes. If we took a "fast"
young nobleman, for instance, and put him to some
office agreeable to himself, so that he conceived a
decided liking to harness, it would do him a deal
more good in the way of reforming him than a course
of lectures on the seventh commandment! And
assuming that by so doing he enticed other "swells"
to buckle on official armour, it might interfere with
the prospects of some who had never been "fast,"
but on the whole, society would benefit by the
change. I maintain that that would be the correct
method to adopt with some of those thieves who are
totally irreclaimable by our present system of prison
discipline. With regard to the casual and petty
thieves, their case is somewhat different. Many of
them could not be raised above the lowest class of

common labourers, but by adopting a system of individualization, that is studying each man's natural abilities, we could always arrive at the best results. It might be advanced as a third objection, that it would be impossible to make thieves pay their expenses in prison, and a fine in addition. Under our present system I admit it would be very difficult, but in the penal workshops, into which I would turn all our prisoners, this objection would not hold good. The prisoner would then be stimulated to labour at paying work agreeable to his tastes and suitable to his abilities, and the cost of his maintenance would be less than it is at present. Those who really could not earn a living in the penal workhouses, and those who would not earn their living, I would transfer to the prison for criminal incurables. I would not have any first offenders against property in prison, I would punish them as ticket-of-leave men. In the penal workshops I would only have persistent thieves. In the convict prisons only great offenders against the person and traitors. All the persistent criminals of the petty class, I would consign to the workhouses; but the character of our workhouses would require to be altered. There are three distinct classes of paupers. (1) Those who have become paupers through no fault of their own. (2) Those who have become paupers through vice; and (3) The vagrant class. I would refuse admission to the workhouse to the first class, just as I would refuse admission to the prison in the penal workshops to first offenders against property. I would treat them, on the family system of out-of-door relief, as the deserving poor. The second class I would admit into the workhouse, and the vagrant class as well, but on the understanding that they did not get out again till they had paid their bill. In short we ought to make our prisons and our workhouses paying concerns, and with the former there need be no difficulty whatever; above all we ought to keep the deserving poor from the other classes, and the regular thieves from those who have only erred once. Every man found guilty of crime who can prove that he has been working at an honest calling up to the time he committed it, should be prevented from mixing with confirmed criminals, or even from going into prison, unless for some great crime against the person for which enforced restitution would not be a sufficient atonement.

CHAPTER XIV.

ASKING pardon of my readers for the rather serious digressions I have made in the preceding chapter, I now return to my narrative.

Shortly after the new regulations were made known to the prisoners, I wrote a letter to my brother, and in this solitary instance I confess in a somewhat ironical strain, and as a matter of course the letter was suppressed. I remember one passage in it was to the following effect: " A new arrangement has lately taken place, which grants to all frequently-convicted prisoners with the same sentence as myself, two years of unexpected remission, so that if they should deal as leniently with me, I shall soon be home." This was an allusion to the repeal of an old regulation whereby convicts who had revoked a former licence were thereby disqualified for receiving any remission from a subsequent sentence. Prisoners, therefore, who had so disqualified themselves, and had been

re-convicted under the old regulation, were quite
unprepared for being placed on the same footing in
all respects as those who had been convicted for the
first time, which was actually the case under the new
regulations. Prisoners conversant with the recom-
mendation of the Royal Commissioners, anticipated
quite a different policy on the part of the authorities.
They expected that men who had succumbed to
strong temptation and who had never been in prison
before would have been more mercifully dealt with;
and that increased severity would have been visited
upon those who had already had several opportunities
of redeeming their character, but had fully proved
their determination to continue in their evil ways;
but the authorities decided otherwise.

About this time there occurred a circumstance which
I must mention:—one of my fellow-prisoners with a deformed foot, asked the medical officer to amputate his
leg below the knee. The request was complied with,
and the patient, who was a very stout fellow, was provided with a mechanical substitute, with springs in
the heel. This man's brother was a professional thief,
and both are still in the same prison under different
names. The artificial leg was altogether unsuitable
for a man in his position in life, inasmuch as he would
not be able to pay the expense of repairing it. That,
however, I had nothing to do with. The leg was
made by a prisoner, and being a nice looking article,

it was exhibited to strangers in the doctor's room for
a considerable time, to show them how kind they
were to the prisoners, and to keep up that system, so
dear to officials, of washing the outside of the platter
for the public gaze, whilst all uncleanliness remained
within.   Another prisoner, who met with an accident
at the public works, and lost his leg in endeavouring
to save an officer's life, arrived at the prison and was
also provided with a mechanical substitute.   Feeling
my health failing me, I thought that an artificial leg,
by enabling me to take exercise, or get into the fields
to work, might save me from again being sent to
hospital; and seeing other prisoners getting them, I
resolved to petition the director for the same favour.
I was further encouraged in my resolution by the fact
that it was a new director who was then inspecting
the prison.   The visiting day arrived, and as before,
I was ushered into the presence of the new official, and
placed between two warders with staves in their
hands.   At the desk sat the new director, by his
side stood the governor, and in front of the desk the
chief warder.

"Well! what do you want?"

I told him that I had lost my leg in prison, that I
was feeling my health giving way, that I was anxious
to be in a position to move about a little better, and
would feel very grateful if he would allow me to
have an artificial leg, the same as the other prisoners

had. The governor endeavoured to deny that any artificial legs had been furnished to prisoners; but being prepared for something of that kind, I gave the particulars I have already mentioned, which were confirmed by the chief warder. The result was, that the director promised to see the doctor on the subject. I was glad to see a disposition on the part of the new director to listen to the prisoner without any attempt to bully him, and became sanguine of the success of my petition. Next visit, however, it was curtly refused on the ground of expense. As it so happened, I was obliged to go to the hospital once more after the lapse of a few weeks, and swallowed as much quinine there as cost far more than an artificial leg, made by a prisoner whose labour at knitting was not worth a penny a day, would have done! The prisoner who lost the deformed leg began to use his artificial substitute, and two or three times it got out of repair. One of these repairs was said to have cost 30s. in London. In the long run it was broken, and an ordinary wooden-peg leg substituted, which was the only one suitable to his position.

I now began to be exceedingly depressed in spirits, and this depression operated prejudicially to my health. I began at this time to string couplets together, as an exercise for my mind and my memory, and so great was the relief which was thus afforded me that I ventured to compose verses in earnest,

M

and succeeded in this way in partially forgetting my troubles. To keep them in my memory was the most difficult task, as it was quite contrary to the prison rules to write one's own compositions in a copy-book. If John Bunyan had been unfortunate enough to get into one of our model prisons, the "Pilgrim's Progress" would have been unwritten. From this time up to the close of my imprisonment I exercised my mind in the manufacture of verses, my stock ultimately amounting to many hundreds of lines, which my memory faithfully retained. My chest having now become very painful and weak, in consequence of so much reading aloud, as I was obliged to do on a somewhat poor diet, I was compelled to enter the hospital a second time, suffering from severe general debility accompanied by a cough, after having been about thirteen months in the prison. On my admission I received a change of diet and tonic medicines. For some weeks I was confined to bed, and not till six months had elapsed was I discharged.

An event took place during my second sojourn in the hospital which caused much excitement among the prisoners. This was the stabbing of a Scripture-reader by one of the patients. The case was afterwards disposed of at the Assizes, and the culprit was sentenced to five years' penal servitude. As his former sentence had as much to ruu, this was considered as a triumph on the part of the prisoner. He committed the crime not with intent to kill, but for the purpose of bringing his case before the public, and of being removed to another prison. He had committed a similar crime before, but the directors had disposed of it privately, so that the particulars of it should not reach the newspapers. In this case to which I refer, the prisoner alleged on his trial that the doctor would not give him treatment for his complaint; he found that it was of no use complaining to a higher authority, that he could not get removed to another prison, nor procure the treatment he had been accustomed to receive for his disease. He was much beyond the ordinary convict in point of ability. He defended himself, cross-examined the authorities, and made some of the chiefs cut very sorry figures under the divining rod. He at last gained his point, for he exposed the authorities and obtained his removal to another prison, where he would have what he considered proper medical treatment—good food being an essential item in the prescription.

After this case occurred the governor was allowed to retire on a pension ; or, in the language of the convicts, " he got the 'sack' in a genteel way," but in reality the doctor was the man on whom the responsibility rested, and it was him the prisoner wished to stab and not the Scripture-reader, but he never could get

M 2

the opportunity. I notice this case chiefly to show
that our present law is inoperative in the case of a
class of prisoners of which this one was a fair type.
He was a sad cripple, walking with the assistance of
two crutches, and dragging his legs behind him ; he
was afflicted with spinal disease and heart complaint;
he had been a convict before, and had lived all the
time like a fighting cock ; commanding medical
treatment, and working only as it suited himself ; he
had nothing to fear in the commission of crime except
being sent to hospital, and his diseases would compel
the majority of doctors to give him good diet, and
good general treatment.   If they had refused or
neglected to do so, the prisoner's life would have been
sacrificed.   Whatever may have been the truth in
his case, he felt and believed that his days were being
shortened, and he was one of those who would rather
have died on the scaffold than submit to a lingering
death in prison.   A short time ago he was found dead
in his cell.   It was asserted that he had taken some
medicine internally which was intended for external
application, and that he had thus poisoned himself ; it was alleged that his object was to make
himself ill in order to obtain better treatment. This
is somewhat doubtful, but as his death took place at
another prison I am unable to give more particulars.
The newspapers having commented rather severely
on this stabbing case, it was deemed necessary by the

prison authorities to have a counter current set in motion. For this purpose an inquest was held on the body of a deceased convict; all the chief authorities were called to this special inquest, and three prisoner-nurses were also examined, and the result appeared in the newspapers, to the great astonishment of the prisoners. It was reported that the coroner had held an inquest on the body of a deceased convict, and found that the deceased had received excellent diet and medical treatment. He further expressed his surprise to find the prisoners received such luxuries in prison as fish, fowl, and jellies, in addition to wines, &c! If they had not mentioned the fish, fowls, and jellies, the prisoners might not have taken much notice of it, but the facts being as follows, it must be confessed that they had some grounds for making uncomplimentary remarks. For thirty-two or thirty-three months previous to the inquest there had been no fowls in the hospital, and there never had been either fish or jellies served out to patients during the whole period the prison had been in existence. Some time after the inquest there were two or three soles cooked for dying prisoners, one of them being a Fenian.

After the arrival of the Fenians and a new priest, there was a considerable alteration in the hospital treatment—fowls became quite common, apple pies, meat pies, and sundry other luxuries being intro-

duced.   Fish and jellies being still wanting, however, to bear out the newspaper report.

I do not wish it to be understood that the Fenians
receive better medical treatment than the other
prisoners, nor is their position generally much better.
They sat at work in the same room with me ; they
had the privilege of exercising by themselves, but
judging from their eagerness for my society and political conversation, they seemed to consider the privilege in the light of a punishment.   One concession
was made to them, however, which at first rather surprised me.   They were allowed to write to their friends
as often, when they were in the third class, as other
prisoners were allowed who were in the first, and the
censorship over their letters was not very severe.
One of the head-centres, and one of the principal
writers and agitators in the would-be rebellious sister
isle was a tall, bony, cadaverous-looking man, afflicted
with scrofula.   He could have ate double his allowance of food, and probably he required more than he
was allowed ; at all events he thought he was not getting proper treatment, and wrote a very strong letter
on the subject to his friends.   This letter was considered a libel on the establishment, but the governor
and director decreed that the letter should pass, as
it would show the Fenians outside that their friends
in prison were not on a bed of roses.   This was acting in quite a contrary direction to that which was

usually followed with the correspondence of other prisoners. Any letter that told of the comforts of the prison, and gave the friends of the prisoner the idea that he was in Paradise was sure to pass, and the writer of it would also get into the good graces of the officials ; but if there was any word of complaint, especially if addressed to any person of influence, the extinguisher was put upon it at once.

I remember one of the patients writing to his friends that he was unwell, but that he really did not know very well what to say about his complaint, as one doctor told him to get out of bed and " knock about," as there was nothing the matter with him, while another told him he was dying, and on no account to leave his bed, and between the two he did not know what to do. This was at the time when the two medical officers seemed to pull against each other. The letter produced an improvement in them, but it was never allowed to reach its destination.

Another case was that of a Quaker's letter (the only one of the creed I met with in prison). He was a quiet old man, and for upwards of three years had been allowed certain trifling privileges on account of his religious opinions,—one of them was his being allowed to sit when grace was said before meals. One day, a young consequential officer happened to be on duty in the ward where the Quaker

was domiciled, and when he called "Attention !" for
grace, the Quaker, as usual, kept his seat.   The
officer ordered him to stand up, and the Quaker
having attempted to explain he was "reported," and
besides being sent to " Chokey," forfeited some of
his remission for the offence.   He wrote to an in-
fluential Quaker in the North of England, explaining
the particulars of the case; but his letter contained
one clause sufficient to condemn it in the eyes of the
prison officials, and it was this, "Be good enough to
send this letter to John Bright, Esq., M.P."

CHAPTER XV.

ON one occasion during my second sojourn in hospital, my attention was accidentally directed to a pale, sickly-looking young man, who had just arrived with a number of other prisoners from Millbank, and whose appearance and manner so unmistakably betrayed the genus to which he belonged that I decided to avail myself of the first opportunity which presented itself of learning his history. It so happened that he was located in the next bed to mine, and I had thus no difficulty in finding an occasion to gratify my curiosity, and the following dialogue took place on the first day of his arrival.

"Well, what news have you brought from Millbank?"

"Oh, nothing particular; the prison's full, and a good many back on their ticket."

"How long have you done?"

"Nine months."

"What's your sentence?"

"Seven years."

"Have you done your separates in the 'bank ?"

"No; in the country—down in Somerset."

"What sort of treatment did you get ?"

"Wretched! They are making it very hot now, and I got 'bashed' as well."

"The flogging has made your health bad, I suppose ?"

"Yes, it made me spit up ever so much blood."

"Were you ever flogged before ?"

"Yes, twice."

"Twice! Why, how old are you ?"

"Twenty-three, and I have done two 'leggings,' and this is my third, besides short bits in the county jails."

"During your first 'legging' I suppose you had been among the boys at the Isle of Wight ?"

"Yes."

"I think most of the Isle of Wight boys get into prison again ? I have seen a great many now who did their first bit there."

"Well, a good many of them went on the cross."

"You belong to London, I suppose ?"

"Yes."

"Did you get your sentence there ?"

"No, in Bristol."

"How long were you out this last time ?"

"Six days, and I was half-drunk all the time."

"How long was your last sentence?"

"Three years, and I did it all."

"How did you lose your remission?"

"For striking a 'screw.'"

"Why did you not remain in London when you went out last?"

"Well, these 'flimping' fellows have alarmed the Londoners so much that there is no chance of getting a living at thieving."

"You mean that the garotters have spoiled your trade by making people more guarded?"

"Why, man, they are wearing steel collars and carrying fire-arms."

"But they have passed a flogging bill in Parliament for all these crimes with violence."

"Flogging be d——d! D'ye think that would stop them? It's the people being always on the watch, and the 'Bobbies' more expert, that makes them afraid of being caught. But I wish they would never try that game, for it gives the 'buzzer' no chance."

"You say you have been flogged three times: how did you like it?"

"The first time I was a kid, and cried like anything; the second time I never uttered a word nor flinched in the least; and the last time, I sang the bawdiest song I could lay my tongue on, and cried, 'Come on, ye ——!'"

"Well, I think you are a very foolish fellow; you have permanently injured your health by your conduct."

"I know all that, but my temper won't let me be quiet; and, by jingo! if this butcher does not treat me properly, I'll make him pay for it; I'll see now what the fish and the fowls and the jellies are like."

"You appear to be consumptive?"

"Yes, second stage."

"Now, take my advice and be as quiet as you can, and you will do very well here."

Well, if these fellows will let me alone, and the 'butcher' gives me good treatment, I'll be all right; but I'll stand no nonsense—there's no two ways with me. Is there any 'snout' knocking about? I have got some money, and if you can tell me how I can get it I will be glad."

"I do not use it myself, but I see others dealing away in it, and I have no doubt that some of these fellows opposite will be able to put you on the right scent."

This was one of the men who bring odium on the whole class of prisoners, and prejudice society against them. He was a thorough-bred professional thief, and, in addition, he was one of the very worst prison characters. His temper was very violent, and at times apparently uncontrollable. The lash had been

tried on him, and, as in every case I met with, in
vain. If he lives to complete the term of his imprisonment he will, as a matter of course, return to
his old practices,—the only method he knows of making his living. The officials were afraid he would
stab or otherwise injure some of them; and he was
petted and indulged a good deal at first. His diet
was changed every other day, until they got tired of
humouring him; and then he got into trouble. At
last, after he had been about eighteen months in the
prison, and had insulted and threatened to strike the
governor, he was suddenly removed to another
prison, where he would no doubt repeat the same
game. In all probability he will be in the grave
before he is due for liberation. Yet with all this, he
could have been *led* like a child; but to attempt to
drive him was out of the question. I confess I was
very glad when he was removed from the bed next
to mine to one further away.

My neighbour on the other side was a very different
character. He was a self-taught artist, and was
gifted with considerable natural genius. His failing
had been intemperance, and his crime a "got up"
case of rape. He was quite a philosopher in his
way, always happy, always contented; nothing came
amiss to him. Imprisonment was of no account with
him; he was above it altogether. He had no inclination to break the law, and was most unlikely to

enter a prison a second time. Yet this prisoner
never could manage to get such good treatment as
the other, simply because he was easily pleased. He
looked upon the prison as a place of passage to
be made the best of, not as a home. He could be
liberated to-morrow with perfect safety to the public,
whilst the other prisoner, who had precisely the same
sentence, will go into the society of thieves, and the
pockets of other people, the moment he is permitted
the opportunity. The artist, although a cripple,
could have earned far more in prison than would have
supported himself if he had been allowed to do so.
The thief could not have supported himself honestly
anywhere, and in prison he was never taught how to
do so.

Now suppose these two men had been sent to a
penal workshop, each with a fine of 50*l.* upon his head,
instead of to a human cage with a seven years' sentence; suppose that they were each debited, in addition to the fine, with the cost of their food, lodging,
&c., and credited with their labour on the profits on
their work, and liberated when the account was
balanced, what would be the result? In all probability it would be this : that the artist, anxious
for liberty, would economise, do with as little food
and drink as possible, exert his faculties to the uttermost, and in a year or two perhaps he would have
paid off the amount of his fine, and the cost of his

maintenance. He would then be liberated in a condition to benefit society; impressed with the folly of his conduct in having thrown away so much time and money, and determined to keep the law for the future.

The tax-payers, instead of being as now burdened to support him, would not only be relieved of that particular grievance, but would have the satisfaction of seeing the criminal contributing large sums to the right side of the public ledger. Instead of paying a quarter of a million of hard and honest-earned money to maintain convict prisons, and ever so much more to the county jails, we might in time make them self-sustaining, and the offenders of the law a source of revenue to the country.

If the casual offender regained his freedom in two years under such a system as I have indicated, when would one of the worst members of the most dangerous class regain his? And what would be his condition and prospects? He would certainly get deeper into debt to begin with, and if thoroughly determined to remain a dangerous and useless member of society he would never regain his liberty. Perhaps he would commit an offence against the person, and bring restraint and punishment upon himself in every way unworthy of unrestrained freedom. But if he were resolved to become an honest and industrious man, the opportunity and the means for so doing would be before him; he would set to and learn a trade, practice economy, confine his hands to his own pockets, prove himself worthy of trust, and at the end of four or five years regain his freedom. He could never keep pace with the other in the race for liberty, nor would he be fitted for the proper use of his liberty until he had practised industry under a natural and healthy stimulus up to the paying point—the point when he becomes convinced in his own mind that honesty is the best policy. His prospects on liberation would then be very different from what they are under the present system. He would then be suited for being a colonist. It would have been proved to his own mind that he could make a living by honest industry, and in most cases this is the all-important consideration. Removed from his old associates, placed in circumstances where money can be made by industry, and still keeping the cost of his transportation against him to be paid out of the first of his own free earnings, society would then have done its duty by him. I wish to impress this strongly on those who take an interest in the subject of criminal reformation; and therefore repeat, that if we can prove to the thief's own satisfaction that he can earn an honest livelihood, at work agreeable to himself and suited to his abilities, we shall do much towards making him an honest man. But, let us starve him and lash him, and tyrannize over him, and we shall send him to the grave or the gallows ; and if we combine statuesque and compulsory Christianity with such treatment, we make him in addition a hardened unbeliever and atheist. And yet hitherto we have sent such men prematurely into the other world, in such condition of soul and body, with as great complacency as if the blame were all their own.

The next case I shall notice was a very different one indeed. The prisoner had been a clergyman in the Church of England for upwards of twenty years, and during that long period had discharged his duties to the satisfaction of his flock and his superiors in the church. I believe he had made an imprudent second marriage. His wife was beneath him in social position and being inclined to habits of extravagance had incurred debts which his small income could not meet. He used funds entrusted to his care by some society for the purpose of liquidating these debts, intending to replace them when his stipend became due. These funds happened, however, to be wanted much sooner than had been customary, he was not able to produce them, and the consequence was penal servitude for a very long period. I could not help pitying the prisoner. He had never rubbed shoulders with the world. An occasional evening with the Squire's family or in the homes of the less exalted among his parishioners,

N

had been almost his only opportunity of gaining a knowledge of life. He was apparently very penitent, and often I noticed him shedding tears (a very unusual sight in a convict prison), and he seemed to feel his degrading and cruel punishment very keenly indeed. He was very kind to the prisoners and was a great favourite with them, and in consequence not in the very best odour with the authorities. He was, like myself, employed as a reader in the work-rooms, but was soon removed to another prison, where he is now employed tailoring ! What will he—what can he do, when liberated ?   I heard of three other clergymen who had been convicts, one of them went abroad after he was liberated, and soon afterwards died. A second went to a part of the country where he thought he would not be known, opened a school which was not very successful, got into good society, and for a time was very comfortable and happy,   One day, however, a cabman who came to drive him to a gentleman's house, recognized him as an old prison companion, and the fact having become known he was obliged soon after to leave the neighbourhood. The third met with a fate somewhat similar.   He happened to be at an evening party, in the house of a friend ; one of the guests would not remain in his company, and to save the party from shipwreck he threw himself overboard into the great ocean of life. Perhaps some friendly fish has swallowed him and cast him on a Christian shore! I never heard of him again. The fate of these men gives rise to many sorrowful reflections; surely there is cruel injustice in the law which condemns a minister of the church of Christ, who in a moment of sore temptation breaks the eighth commandment, to years of slavery and a life of degradation and disgrace, compared with which death itself would be mercy and kindness, and yet permits constant and flagrant violations of the seventh, by rich and titled transgressors, to be compromised with gold! Why do we in the one case brand the offender with the mark of Cain, and in the other cover with a golden veil both sin and sinner? If it is necessary, "as a warning to others," that casual violations of the eighth commandment should be so punished, why is it unnecessary to warn others against the frequent and habitual violation of the seventh? Would the payment of money, together with the loss of character, social position, &c., not be a sufficient warning to all men in a position to commit such acts of dishonesty as may be included under the general designation of breaches of trust? But what does so-called justice now demand in such cases? Let ten clergymen embezzle 100*l.* each, and hear how society indemnifies itself for the crime and the loss! By the mouth of one judge, one of these clergymen is sentenced to one year in prison; by the mouth of another judge, another of these clergymen is sentenced to two years in prison; by the mouth of a third, another is condemned to three years penal servitude, to labour and associate with the dregs of society; by the mouth of a fourth, four years of such humiliation; and so on.

Are all these just judges;—or is only one of them just? and which is he?

These are questions I will leave my readers to answer for themselves. Of one thing I am satisfied, that our present laws on the subject require alteration.

CHAPTER XVI.

QUACKERY—FOOD—A CHATHAM PRISONER EATS SNAILS AND FROGS—
SIR JOSHUA JEBB'S SYSTEM AND ITS DEFECTS.

I HAVE already said in a previous chapter that our prison authorities regard the convicts as mere human machines, all made after the same model, and that the machinery, by some abnormal defect in its original construction constantly impels them in the wrong direction. In official eyes they do not appear to be men having peculiarities of physical construction and constitution, individuality of character, or to have been so designed as to be like other men, moulded by circumstances, or amenable to the influence of education or social position. They look at him through the official spectacles, the lenses of which are carefully adjusted so that the object shall present not only a perfectly uniform appearance but also appear uniformly bad. If the convict is in good health, the machinery working smoothly—but still by the defect in its construction always in the wrong direction—there are the regulation appliances, not for remedying the original

defect in the machinery, it must be remembered, and
if possible getting it to work in the *right* direction,
but appliances to check, thwart, and by force drive it
backward, which in most cases it cannot and will not
do, and breakages, ruin of machinery and other
appliances also are the only result. They number
and ticket the convict according to his sentence,
range them all up, count them eleven times a day and
say to them, " Convicts, now here you are, all ticketed
and counted, all of you are afflicted with some moral
disease, we are here to cure you, and we have *one*
pill which will do it, and you must swallow it."

This is the perfection of penal legislation at which,
after many royal commissions, and much parliamentary eloquence, we have arrived !   One would
have imagined that a gigantic quackery and multi-
tudes of quack doctors could have been procured and
set in motion with less trouble and at less expense !
Only on one point there is universal agreement, let
the machine be working either in the right direction
or the wrong—so long as it is working it must be
oiled, that is a necessity of machine-life, so to speak
—the man or convict must be *fed*. But how feed
him ?   To you, my reader, and I, the natural
answer would be that the machine must be oiled, or
the man fed, in greater or less proportion to the
power and capacity of the machine or man, and to
the amount of work we require from it or him.   But

we are both wrong. Our prison authorities say, "Machine, big or little, you shall all have exactly the same quantity of oil, neither more nor less. You little machines there, with oil running all over you, how smoothly and uncomplainingly you work! You big machines, you may creak as you please, your journals may get hot, blaze up and produce universal smash: but you can't get any more oil; we can't allow you to lick up any of that which is running over your little neighbour there—that is for the pigs, and for *us.*" Is not this amazing folly? Or again, suppose we were to take a race-horse, a dray-horse, a farmer's horse, a broken-down hack, and a Shetland horse—for these more nearly resemble the various classes of convicts—and say to them, "Horses, you have all offended the laws of horsedom, and stand fully convicted of clover stealing. For this most heinous crime you are each condemned to draw a load, one ton weight, fifteen miles every day—Sundays excepted —for five years, and your allowance of food will be two feeds of oats, and one allowance of hay per diem;" and what would be the result, supposing that the allowance of hay and oats was just barely sufficient for the average—say the farmer's horse?

First of all the race-horse, able to eat his oats and a portion of the hay, could do with some additional dainty bits, perhaps, but on the whole he has his stomach filled and can live. He is yoked to his load, and being a spirited animal, he goes at it very hard, succeeds for a time; at last he sticks in a rut, puts on a "spurt," and breaks down. He can't do the work. He is put down at six marks a day, or no remission. He is spoiled for ever, and as a racer his days are ended.

The dray-horse comes next, the load is a mere toy to him, he gets his eight marks a day, but by-and-bye he begins to feel the effects of an empty stomach, to fill which he would require double the allowance of food he receives; and in the long run he too breaks down and is passed into the hands of the veterinary surgeon, and is ruined as a useful animal.

Next comes the farmer's horse, and the load and diet being suitable to him, he can do the punishment and easily satisfy the law.

The broken-down hack is never yoked at all, he passes into the hands of the surgeon, and there remains. While the little Shetlander is in clover; he never had so many oats before—has actually as much again as he can consume—and the cart and harness being too large, and the load altogether ridiculous for his strength, he is never put to it, and so escapes the legal punishment. And so it is that one portion of the inhabitants of horsedom, pointing to the Shetlander, cry out that "the convicts have too much food, they are up to the eyes in luxuries;" another portion, pointing to the dray horse, say "the convicts

are starved, and are dying of hunger;" whilst a third
answers both by pointing to the farm horse and
saying that " he can do the work and satisfy the law.
Why should they not all be treated alike ? a horse is
a horse all the world over."

Our system of dieting and working convicts is
exactly similar to the above ; only at the invalid
prison where I was confined the law was not adhered
to. I knew prisoners who ate double the quantity
of food allowed them, and I knew others who did
not eat above half. Sometimes it happened that a
voracious prisoner could not get his food exchanged
so as to increase its bulk, and in that case he would
be compelled to seek refuge in hospital. If the diet
there was not sufficient, God help him, for from man
no further aid was to be expected.

I recollect having a conversation with a prisoner
who had just arrived with eighteen others from the
prison at Chatham. He had got his leg broken
accidentally while at work there, and the medical
men had not made a very good job of putting the
bones together, so that he did not expect ever to be
able to use it. I asked him what sort of a place
Chatham was under the new system.

"Oh, it's the worst station out," he replied, "they
are starved and worked to death. They are even
eating the candles, and one man died lately who had
twenty or thirty wicks in his stomach when the *post*

mortem took place. In the docks I have seen fellows
pick up the dirtiest muck you ever saw, and swallow
it! There are lots of fellows there who eat all the
snails and frogs they can get hold of. I have seen
one man several times swallow a live frog as easily
as you could bolt an oyster. Frogs and snails are
considered delicacies at Chatham."

"How did you get on with the food yourself?"

"Well, I was never much of an eater, and I could
get on middling well with it; but then the food was
better there than it is here. This is the worst station
out for 'grub.' The cook and steward must be d——
villains to rob a lot of prisoners of their food."

"Do they all get eight marks a day at Chatham?"

"No, not nearly all; many only get seven, and
some not more than six. The 'screws' there are ——
tyrants, and if they don't mind what they are about
some of them will get murdered. There are a few
fellows there would rather be 'topt' than be messed
about in such a way, and have to die in prison at
last. What sort of 'screws' have you here?"

"Well, the majority of them are very civil fellows;
there are a few, perhaps, inclined to exceed their
duty, but on the whole they are not bad, and you
will have yourself to blame if you get into trouble.
Bad masters make bad servants, and I have no doubt
the Chatham officers are merely carrying out the
directors' orders when they tyrannise over the men."

"What sort of a doctor is this you have got here? he gets a very bad name."

"Well, he is blamed for not giving prisoners treatment until they are just dying, but I do not pretend to be a judge of such matters myself. My advice to you is to be civil and grateful, and do not bother him about food. Do not ask him for anything, just tell him exactly how you feel, and you may do very well here."

The prediction as to the murdering of some of the officers made above by the prisoner was shortly after verified, and the culprit was hanged at Maidstone quite recently. At the Yorkshire prison they had what appeared to me a more sensible method of apportioning the diet. The prisoners were weighed once a month, and if any of them lost weight they were allowed an additional quantity of dry bread to make it up. In the Surrey prison the practice of exchanging and trafficking in food amongst the prisoners counteracted the evils that would otherwise have resulted from the regulations being strictly adhered to; and in the Scottish prisons the use of tobacco appeared to have the same effect. While on the subject of diet, I may allude to a rule which had a very bad effect on the minds of the prisoners who expected justice at the hands of the officials. In the dietary scale brought out in 1864, it was specified that when a prisoner had been two years in prison, he

would be permitted to have the option of tea and two
ounces of bread in lieu of the oatmeal gruel for
supper, and when he had been three years in prison
he might have roasted or baked meat in lieu of
boiled. The convicts sentenced under the old Act
were placed in the first or lowest grade in the scale
of the Act of 1864, but were denied the option of
those changes of diet which were permitted under
it, and which were considered necessary for the
preservation of their health by the medical authorities. The consequence was, and is, that there
were prisoners with life sentences who had been
ten, twelve, and sixteen years in prison on a diet
inferior to those who had only been in prison two
years. No tea and bread at night for them, and
no roasted meat. This regulation was considered
unjust by the prisoners, who said, very naturally,
"They took us off the good diet allowed by the old
Act under which we were sentenced, and placed us
on the lowest scale of the new dietary, and now,
after being two years on the diet we ought not to
have been put on at all, we are not even allowed the
changes open to other prisoners. It is scandalous,
after being ten or twelve years in prison, to see other
prisoners who have only just commenced their time
much better off than we are," &c.

Another grievance the prisoners had, of which
they loudly complained. It was the custom at the

Home Office to forward the prisoners' licenses to the prison once a month, but as a rule these documents were ten days—sometimes three weeks—later than they ought to have been. If a prisoner had earned his marks, and was due for his license, say on the 1st of March, he expected the authorities would keep faith with him, and that his license would arrive on the day it was due. Whatever the convict may be himself, he expects a good example and honourable fulfilment of the engagements on the part of the authorities. In this, however, he was often disappointed, and many a million curses were heaped upon them in consequence. And after all can we wonder at a convict being exasperated if, as it often happened, he had written to a wife, or a father, or brother or sister to meet him on a certain day at the railway station, when he was due for his liberty, and then was disappointed and had to wait a fortnight or three weeks before he could see his friends? This neglect on the part of the authorities at the Home Office, had the effect of making all those who were due for liberation early in the month quite regardless of the prison regulations, as one short sentence would not have made any difference to them under the circumstances.

In Sir Joshua Jebb's day anything of this kind seldom happened. The prisoner's chief grievance then was the robbery of his food by the officers, and as the discipline was lax a mutiny would be the result. This had a good effect for a short time, and as long as the attention of the press was directed to the question, but matters soon became as bad as ever, and it was not until the subject came before the criminal courts that there was any improvement. The name of Sir Joshua Jebb is still held in great veneration by the convict, but as the duty of carrying out his system was entrusted to men of a totally opposite character, it was impossible for it to succeed. Independent, however, of its moral administration, it had defects inherent in itself. No penal bill will suit all moral complaints, and the sooner we depart from quackery the better it will be for the prisoner and the nation as well. Sir Joshua Jebb's system entered too largely into competition with our workhouses and county jails. The prisoners were never taught suitable trades, they were no doubt supplied with food in abundance, and with some opportunities of learning to be industrious and for improving their minds, but they were completely surrounded by far more powerful counter-influences. Even the higher officials carried on a system of wholesale robbery, and winked at the very large retail business done in the same line by the prisoners and under officials. At Bermuda and Dartmoor convict establishments I believe there were more crimes committed by officers and prisoners together than the prisoners

could or would have committed if they had been at
liberty. Prisoners could do very much as they
liked in those days, and the consequence was that the
"roughs," or the worst characters, gave the "ton" to
the whole prison. A country bumpkin who had
stolen a bag of potatoes, perhaps, soon learned the
theory of picking pockets and the art of garotting
in these places, and being unequal to the former he
would adopt the latter as a means of earning a livelihood. Another cause of the increase in the number
of garotting cases, was the conduct of the directors
who visited the prisoners and punished the prisoners.
Their injustice and incivility to prisoners bore a striking contrast to the mild and dignified civility of Sir
Joshua their chief. I have known prisoners return
from the presence of a director, foaming with inward
rage at being bullied out of the room and punished
without being permitted to utter a word in their own
defence. In many of these cases I have known the
prisoners to be innocent. Such men would go out of
prison vowing vengeance on some one, and ready for
any deed of darkness that might tempt them. I do not
wonder that they took to garotting when I reflect
upon their character and the treatment they received
in prison. Prisoners seldom, if ever, vow vengeance
against a judge or a magistrate; the objects of their
wrath are some policeman who has sworn falsely, or
some other witness who has committed perjury or

betrayed them ; and we may naturally seek to inquire why the prison judge is not as favourably regarded as his learned brother who holds open court ? I believe the reason is this, that a prison director can starve and flog and retain prisoners in confinement for years, according to the length of their respective remissions, and none but those directly interested in full and quiet prisons know anything about it. If the governor and directors of prisons had to dispense justice in presence of a reporter for the press, how great would be the reformation immediately effected. To the prisoner it would also be welcome, for if it ensured him of nothing else but civility it would be a boon. A civil word goes a long way with a convict, and it is so seldom he gets one from the chiefs of prisons that he is apt to place a value upon it beyond its real worth.

CHAPTER XVII.

A NEW GOVERNOR—BREAD-AND-WATER JACK—SEVERE PUNISHMENTS—
DIRECTORS AGAIN—A HERB DOCTOR—EXTRAORDINARY STORY.

DURING my second stay in hospital the governor
from another prison came to rule over our
establishment. He was known to most of the prisoners as " Bread and Water Jack," some called him
"Captain Spooney," some " the Lurcher," and others
" Mr. Martinet." The patients had just completed
their out-of-door exercise, and were standing in file
two deep when he first made his appearance. Some
of the prisoners whispered, " That's the new governor,"
and the sound having reached his official ear, the order
was issued "Now you men, you must understand there
is to be no talking in the ranks when I pass you."
Almost every week some fresh order issued from the
new governor, and the following may be taken as a
fair example of the weighty matters which troubled
the official head, and afford a very good idea of its
qualifications for disposing of them.

" Prisoners must roll their neckerchiefs twice round

o

their necks and tie them in a particular way," and the way is then described.

" Prisoners must walk three abreast round the parade, and not pass each other in walking."

" Prisoners must be sure to keep their hands out of their pockets in the coldest days."

" Prisoners must not neglect to salute the governor when he passes them."

" Prisoners must walk only two abreast instead of three abreast, as formerly ordered."

" The spoons and platters must be placed in this particular way." And next week the order came to have the spoons and platters placed in exactly the opposite way !

" Prisoners' hair must be cropped shorter; they must not go to bed so soon as they have done : they must cease talking at work," and so on.

These were the principal orders issued, and attempted to be carried out. I say attempted, for some of them were regularly evaded or broken by the prisoners, and winked at by the officers. These were the orders that were expected to be instrumental in converting thieves into honest men ! Whatever opinion might be formed of their probable efficacy out of doors, or of the sanity of the man who sat in his office and scrawled them out, the thieves themselves mocked and ridiculed them, and called the small-minded military man set over them a

" Barmey "* humbug. " What does it matter," they
would say to each other, " how we walk ? What does it
matter whether our neck-ties be once or twice round ?
Why don't they teach us to get an honest living and
show us a good example ? What good will all this
humbugging do us ? We don't want to come into such
places if they will only let us live when we are out.
Why don't they find us work and try to keep us
out of prison ?" " Ah ! that would spoil their own
trade," someone would reply. Such criticisms
passed between the prisoners on these new orders,
with an accompaniment of oaths which I cannot
repeat.

The punishment for prison offences now became
more severe under the new governor, and the following may be taken as fair examples of the manner in
which this class of offenders were dealt with. A
convict just about due for his liberation had half-an-
inch of tobacco given him by another prisoner. The
officer happened to notice the gift, went to the prisoner, found the contraband article upon him, and
took him before the governor. That gentleman
sentenced him to ten days in the refractory cells, and
recommended him to the prison director for the loss
of his gratuity and three months' remission. The
unfortunate prisoner was by-and-bye called up and
informed that in addition to the governor's sentence

* Insane.

o 2

he was condemned to lose all his gratuity money, which amounted to about 3*l*., and three months of his remission. Two sentences for one offence were getting very common, but this prisoner happened to be one of those who cared very little about liberty, and received the information very coolly. As soon as he was out of the cells he had his "snout" again as usual, but he was "chaffed" a good deal by his "pals" for neglecting to swallow the quid when he saw the officer coming to him. One of the hospital nurses (a convict) got punished, though not quite so severely, for appropriating to his own use a mutton chop that he was ordered to carry to the pigs. At that time the authorities kept swine, who got all the food the patients could not eat, but now it is sold. The prisoner thought, I presume, that the chop would do a hungry man more good than it would an over-fed pig. Another prisoner was sentenced twice for having an onion on his person. One of his fellow-prisoners who was working among these luxuries gave him one, and as the officer in charge had a grudge against him, he was taken before the governor, who gave him ten days' punishment, to which the director afterwards considerately added three months! Such offences as these were of daily occurrence, but the punishments for them when detected were very unequal.

It is not often a convict is flogged, but it does

happen occasionally. I remember a young rollicking Irishman being flogged for attempting to strike an officer, who, as often happens, was far more to blame than the prisoner, who in this case was goaded and tempted to strike. The majority of the officers—who are civil and sensible men, considering their position in society—would have acted very differently.

Another case, where the prisoner not only attempted but did actually strike his warder rather severely, met with a more lenient punishment. In this case the prisoner was decidedly to blame, and his punishment, in technical language, was " six months in chokey with the black dress and slangs."

These cases were usually disposed of by the director at his monthly sitting. That gentleman—who was fond of having nothing to do—generally spent about twenty-four hours in prison per annum, spread over eleven visits of an average duration of two hours each. Latterly it was rather difficult for a prisoner to get to see him, and quite impossible if he had a complaint to make against any of the officials, which they thought he could establish. I have often thought that this gentleman's duties could be performed more satisfactorily for a less salary than one thousand pounds per annum !

Before leaving the hospital, I will now relate a few of the conversations I had with some of the patients.

" How long have you been unwell ?"

"About fifteen months."

"What is the matter with you?"

"Oh! my health has been ruined by the treatment I received in the Scotch prison before trial."

"How long were you detained waiting trial?"

"Six months."

"Have you been to the public works?"

"Yes, I was at Chatham; but my strength and constitution gave way, and for a working man I am now ruined for life."

"Did you enjoy your health before you got into prison?"

"I was never a day unwell, and was as stout and as fit for work as any man in the country."

"What will you do when you get out of prison?"

"God knows! I suppose I shall have to go to the workhouse. I am very willing to work, but if I don't mend I shall never be able to handle a tool again."

Another case—

"How long have you been ailing?"

"Ten months."

"What is the matter with you?"

"Oh! I am dying fast. I was seven months in a Scotch jail before trial, and that is what is killing me."

This prisoner died a few days after he uttered

these words. His last hours were spent in humming over a Scotch ballad he had learnt when a child.

Another case—

" Well, what's your sentence ?"

" Five years."

" How old are you ?"

" Twenty-five.

" What did you do outside ?"

" I was born in a workhouse, and lived in it for thirteen years, and I have now been nine years in prison; so that I have not had much liberty to do anything at all."

" What do you intend doing when you get out this time ?"

" I think I shall go hawking bits of things through the country."

" I am afraid you will find it difficult to make a living at hawking ?"

" Well I have the prison to come to, where I'll always get my grub."

This prisoner had a delicate constitution, and in his case "hard labour" was a meaningless sentence, and imprisonment was no punishment to him whatever. To have made it more severe would have been all the same to him, as the hospital would then have been his perpetual abode. Some prisoners were in hospital nearly the whole of their sentence. One prisoner lay in bed with paralysis upwards of four years, and had to be lifted out to have his bed arranged several times a day : if he had been paid to commit a crime he could not have done it.

Another prisoner was in hospital all the years I was in prison, and had been so for several years previous to my arrival. I only remember his being in bed a few days on one occasion. I was much interested in another patient, who ultimately died in prison, and whose history was rather a singular one. I shall narrate it as he gave it to me :—

"I am what is called a herbalist, or herb doctor. I was brought up in a workhouse, my parents having died when I was quite a child. I had a great many brothers and sisters, all of whom died young. I had a very delicate constitution, and was thought at one time to be dying of the same disease as carried off my mother and sisters. The doctors gave me up as being beyond their skill. Well, I had begun to study medical botany by this time, and I at last discovered herbs that cured me. I now thought of curing others, and began first with some children belonging to poor people. I succeeded in almost every case, and as I charged nothing at all for the medicines, I was called out by all the poor people in the neighbourhood.

" At last my practice began to interfere with my employment as a weaver, and my master told me that he was willing to keep me and advance my wages, but I was on no account to have anything more to do in curing the sick. Well, I went round my circle of friends to ask their advice, and they unanimously agreed to support me among them rather than be deprived of my assistance. I accordingly gave up my place and opened a herb shop. I studied the properties of herbs constantly. I had no taste for any other employment. I tried the effects of all of them on myself first of all, and sometimes on my wife, before I decided on using them, and I daresay I may have done too much in this way in order to be able to assure my patients that I had first taken a dose myself. I have read all the books on the subject, in addition to my own practical experience; and I will not yield the palm to anyone for having a knowledge of herbs—I mean as to their medical properties. Well, I continued in my first shop for about nine years, got married, and had a comfortable home. About this time a clergyman of my acquaintance happened to be removing to another county, a considerable distance from the town where I lived, and as I had cured his wife after all the regular doctors had given the case up as hopeless, he offered me 52*l.* per annum if I would go to the same place as he was removing to and open a shop there, and I agreed. I was unfortunate the first year in not getting many patients, and began to regret that I had left my old abode. But by-and-bye the news of my cures spread abroad in the neighbourhood, and I soon had as many patients as I could attend to. I never advertised a line, and yet I had patients as far away as Scotland. Ultimately my patients extended to the middle classes, and that was what brought me here. So long as I confined my labours to the poor, the regular doctors did not interfere with me, but when I began to take away their paying patients by the half-dozen, they tried all they could to damage my character, and get me out of the district."

"What is your sentence ?"

" Seven years, and I'll tell you how I got it. I sold a mixture composed of four different herbs, which is the most effectual medicine for certain diseases peculiar to females; in fact, it is invaluable to young unmarried women subject to the complaint I refer to, but, unfortunately for me, it has also the effect of procuring abortion. Well, one day a young woman came to me and wished to purchase some of this medicine. I had cured an unmarried female of her acquaintance, but before giving her the medicine I cautioned her not to take it if she was *enciente*, as it would procure abortion. The female who now applied to me wished it for that very purpose; her husband was a sailor, she had been faithless in his absence, and she now wished to keep him in igno- rance of her sin. All this, however, I learned only when too late. I refused to sell the woman the medicine, as I could see she was married. On being refused, she went to an old woman whose daughter had taken the medicine, and offered her 3*l.* if she would get her some of it. Of course, I was not aware of this when the old woman came to me and asked me for some more of the medicine for her daughter, as she said. I sold her the medicine, which she gave to the sailor's wife. It had the desired effect, and she was well and going about in a couple of days. Her husband now returned, and the old woman demanded the 3*l.*, which the sailor's wife refused to pay. Determined not to be beaten, she went to the husband and told him all about it. He called in doctors to report on the case, which they did, adding that instruments had been used, which was altogether false. The medicine was easily traced to me. Where I was wrong was, in not having a written statement from everyone to whom I sold the herbs, in order to have protected myself against any such charge as was now brought against me. The doctors, no doubt, believed that instruments had been used, because they do not know the particular herbs at all, and no one in England knows them but myself and I do not intend to let many know either—it's dangerous knowledge; but, as God is my judge, I never used it wilfully except for the relief of a disease that carries thousands of our countrywomen to the grave

in the very prime of youth. I have been called to
cases over and over again, after all the doctors had
given them up, and I have often restored the pale
hectic young woman, in an advanced stage of consumption, to health and vigour, by the simple use of
herbs—the best of God's gifts to man !"

"What diseases were you most successful with ?"

"There is one disease I could never cure, and that's
ossification of the heart, but in the great majority of
other diseases I succeeded wonderfully. Sometimes,
of course, I would be called to a consumptive patient
within a few days or hours of his death, when life
was so low as to render it impossible for the medicine
to be taken."

"What do you think of the cold-water system and
homœopathy?"

"The cold water may do for some diseases and for
some patients only, but it is nonsense to think to cure
all diseases in one way. I am not a quack. In
America there are colleges for teaching my system
of curing disease, regular teachers of medical botany.
As for homœopathy, I think very little of it. I have
known it succeed in cholera cases sometimes, however,
as well as the allopathy. When patients have very
little the matter with them, homœopathy, or any
other 'pathy' they have confidence in, does all very
well, and it fills the purses of the practitioners, but
when real rooted disease has to be encountered, the

herbs that God has given for the use of man are the only trustworthy means by which to effect a cure. To give you an idea how many are 'gulled,' I may say robbed, by regular doctors, I will give you the particulars of two cases which happened within my own personal knowledge. Two men were seized with the same fever, and to all appearance the patients were about equal in health, strength, and age. I was called to one, and a regular doctor to the other. The doctor allowed the fever to come to its height, as it is called. He made frequent visits, ran up as large a bill as he thought would be duly paid, and in three or four weeks the patient was at his employment. My patient was at his work in three days, and all it cost him was a few shillings!"

" How did you manage to cure him so speedily ?"

"I never allow fevers to come to the height; I strike at the root of the disease. If you were going to build up a house that was out of repair and encumbered with rubbish, you would naturally clear away the rubbish first and then begin your repairs. Well, that is just how I go to work with disease. Every pore of the skin must be cleansed, opened, and stimulated to action. The stomach must be thoroughly emptied and cleansed by a particular herb, and the bowels must be effectually treated in the same way. The house cleansed, I begin my repairs, which consist in aiding Nature with the most powerful assistance given us by Nature's God for that purpose, and the work is soon completed. I would undertake to cure 100 out of the 150 patients here in a fortnight."

"Do you think you could cure yourself?"

"If I had two herbs here I could prolong my days for a long time, I most thoroughly believe, but they can never touch my disease the way they go on here —I am dying by inches."

This prisoner (now dead) was quite an enthusiast about herbs, and succeeded in imparting confidence in his abilities to the officers as well as the majority of the prisoners. He was to all appearance a man of good principles, and a Christian. How far his own statements regarding his crime can be relied on, I cannot say, but that he succeeded in raising himself from being a poor weaver to be a money-making and successful herb doctor, I know to be correct. I have noticed his case chiefly in order to remark that he turned a good many of the prisoners into pill sellers and incipient quacks, but he never would tell them about the abortion medicine although he gave them prescriptions for almost all diseases. I saw them all, and know the herbs had at least the merit of being innocent. Had he been less honest, and had the herbs which he prescribed been poisonous, I fancy that a good many of Her Majesty's faithful, loyal, and gullible subjects would, long ere now, have returned to the dust from whence they sprang.

CHAPTER XVIII.

IN PRISON AGAIN—I SEE THE PRISON DIRECTOR FOR THE LAST TIME—
GENTLEMEN-PRISONERS—A WILL FORGER—"A WARNING TO OTHERS"
—FENIANS—TREATMENT OF POLITICAL PRISONERS—ANOTHER JAIL-
BIRD.

HAVING recruited my strength in hospital, I was
again discharged to resume my work in prison.
Shortly after my return to my old quarters, I thought
I would inform my friends that some of the companions I met with at the commencement of my
prison career, who had longer sentences than I had,
had been fortunate enough to obtain their liberty,
and, in addition, a free passage to Western Australia
—which was worth about 20*l.*—and that I wished
them to try and do something to aid me in my race
for liberty. But my letter was again suppressed, and
not being able by this means to inform my friends of
my wishes, I entered my name once more as being
desirous to see the director. I anticipated meeting
the regular visiting director, who very rarely refused
a prisoner the privilege of writing a petition to the
Home Secretary, if he had allowed the usual time

(twelve months) to elapse since he had obtained the privilege before. But I was even in this doomed to disappointment, and instead of the director I expected to see, I found myself confronted by the old sinister-looking friend I had been introduced to on a former occasion. I told him on making my humble request that I had not petitioned the Home Secretary for several years, that, in fact, I had not petitioned on the merits of my case at all, and that I would feel grateful if he would extend to me the privilege, usually granted to all well-conducted prisoners, of petitioning the Home Secretary.

Conscience did not seem to be utterly powerless within him, for his eyes would not meet mine, they remained fixed on the desk before him ; but his head shook, and his lips muttered, "No." I pleaded for a moment in beseeching tones which might have softened a heart of stone, but Bassanio's appeal to Shylock was not more futile than mine to him. The words and gesture with which my suppliant attitude was spurned, roused all the manhood in me, and for an instant I felt as if I were a free man and addressing my equal, and in language at once dignified and firm, I requested a sheet of paper that I might appeal to the Board of Directors. My altered mien and tone of voice, so unexpected, so unusual in that secret court, arrested him ; his hand trembled, he looked as Felix might have done when he first heard of

"righteousness, temperance and judgment to come."
My request was granted, and my last interview with
a prison director had come and gone. Two days
afterwards I wrote a letter to the board of directors,
in suitable language, and addressed to the chairman
of the board, preferring my request. Month after
month passed away, but I waited for a reply in vain.
At one time I would have felt both surprised and
annoyed that no notice had been taken of my letter,
but now I knew that I had only experienced the
usual treatment which prisoners receive who have
justice on their side. I had now made three, and
only three requests to the officials during my prison
career, and all these had been denied, and I resolved
to prefer no more. I gave my mind healthy exercise
in the composition of verses, when I was not otherwise employed, and to a great extent forgot my
troubles in my puny flight to obtain a sight of the
poets' mountain.

The last year of my imprisonment was marked by
the arrival of a number of Fenians, and the departure
for freedom of one or two of the very few prisoners
whose society had been a pleasure to me. One of
these had been the editor and proprietor of an in-
fluential country newspaper, and his crime was very
similar to my own. He was a man of deep thought,
and far, very far, from being a criminal at heart.
He was the best educated man I met with in prison,

P

and eminently qualified for writing a treatise on the prevention of crime. The other had been in business in London, and had brought up a large and respectable family. Having been accustomed to mix in the society of some of the most eminent of the city merchants and bankers, his company in such a place as a prison was a great acquisition. After the departure of these two prisoners I had only one intimate and intelligent companion left. His case excited my sympathy, inasmuch as he was a very humble and penitent man, with a sentence of penal servitude for life. A sentence, I believe, inflicted not so much for the crime, but on account of the position the prisoner formerly occupied in society, and "as a warning to others." This is a formula which, in many cases, is made to sanction monstrous injustice, and in all cases, I may say, is practically inoperative. The only parties warned by the fall and punishment of such an one as the prisoner I here refer to, are those in the same respectable position in life, because they are the only parties who have it in their power to commit the same crime. The punishment cannot warn those who are not in and cannot attain to the position which makes the crime possible, and who could not find the opportunity to commit it, even if they were paid to seek it; then why punish such men as this prisoner the more severely, because he was in that position ?

I know it is urged in opposition to that view, that such men ought to know better, that they have no excuse, and so on, but we must bear in mind that all who do wrong know it, the poor and the ignorant as well as the rich and educated, unless they are of unsound mind. Then again, do those in a good position in society require more warning than those who have no character or position to lose ? It would be difficult, I think, for anyone to maintain that position ! The fact is, that conviction merely, without any subsequent punishment at all, would be a much more effective warning to the former class than the gallows even would be to the latter ! The thief plies his trade while the scaffold frowns overhead, it does not deter him, but the lynx eye of a policeman would, even although the penalty was a months' imprisonment instead of the rope. As I have already more than once asserted, it is the fear of *being caught* that deters the thief, and this fear increases and intensifies as we ascend the social ladder; in the case of all first offenders of the law, the punishment is an after-thought, and on that account, as well as on higher grounds, we ought to temper justice with mercy in dealing with all first offenders, more especially with those who offend against property only.

In the case of the prisoner referred to, his crime would not have enriched him more than about twenty pounds, had he succeeded in escaping detection. He committed will-forgery, and of course although the amount was small, still it was a great crime, but I think there might be other methods found for punishing such crimes than dooming the man who commits them to perpetual slavery. I take no notice of the fact that the prisoner in this case maintained his innocence, I assume that he was guilty, and I consider his sentence to be unjust and inexpedient. It is true that this man once sat on the bench and dispensed justice himself; it is also true that he once entertained the Queen of Great Britain in his own house, and these facts to some extent determined the severity of his sentence; I find in them additional reasons for leniency, inasmuch as only a very feeble warning is necessary to prevent men in the position he occupied, and exposed to the same temptation, from following in his steps.

I may now refer to the Fenians, of whom there were six who came to the prison during the last year of my incarceration. They formed a class of prisoners quite distinct from all the others, and their crime being also essentially different, the observation I have made with reference to the proper treatment of ordinary criminals do not apply to them. In the phraseology of the convicts, they were a "rum lot."

They took rank between the "Aristocs," and the "Democrats," and formed an "Irish Brigade." One

of them died soon after his arrival : two of them
were head-centres, and enthusiastic in the rebel
cause, another was a literary man, Irish to the back-
bone, but ready to write for money on any side of
politics. The remaining two were soldiers : one an
American infidel, who cursed Catholics and Fenians
alike for getting him into trouble.. He called the
Pope, the King-of-the-beggars ; quarelled with the
literary Fenian on the subject of religion, and true to
his profession, enforced his arguments by giving his
opponent what the convicts called a punch in the
ear-hole, and extracting the claret from the most prominent feature in his "counting-house." According
to the literary man, Ireland had one great grievance,
and if that were remedied the Emerald Isle would
grow greener than ever. "It is a splendid country,'
he said " for growing tobacco, and if the Irish were
allowed to grow that fashionable weed they would be
the most prosperous of peoples." A vulgar Scotchman
suggested that Ireland would be all right if the Irish
were "Scotched," and the Fenians all roasted on a
gridiron. The irascible Irishman replied that a Scotchman was the incarnation of impudence—and hereupon
a war of words ensued, until the officers' attention
was attracted and brought it to an abrupt conclusion.
The two head-centres appeared to be intelligent men,
but very unlikely to raise the standard, or maintain
the dignity of an Irish Republic.

One of them was said to be their ablest writer, but the other appeared the most loyal and enthusiastic Fenian of them all.

With respect to the punishment of political offenders, the system of restitution which I have advocated would not be suitable, nor would imprisonment in the county prisons answer well. I should not object to government acting as jailers over such men, but they ought to be confined in a prison where they could exercise all their faculties for their own support, and their sentences should be the " Queen's pleasure." Some of those in prison might be liberated at once, others not until the rebellion had been completely extinguished; and the government, not the judge, should regulate the period of their confinement. It may be said that the government have power to liberate such men now, when they choose, which is true enough, but suppose that the rebellion lasts, or breaks out afresh in four or five years, and one of the most dangerous members of the fraternity becomes due for his liberation, they have no power to retain him. This power they ought to possess in all cases where the sacrifice of human life has been perpetrated, attempted, or contemplated. I would not allow this exceptional treatment of political prisoners to interfere, however, with the fundamental principle I have laid down of making all our prisons self-supporting.

I return to my numerous companions, the "regular" convicts, and the following specimens of some of them whom I met during my last months in prison may not be uninteresting. One day I opened the conversation with a regular jail-bird, who had promised me some particulars of his history some time before.

"Well, you promised to give me a little bit of your history this morning, are you ready to begin?"

"Oh! I don't know where to begin, and I have seen so many ups and downs, or rather so many downs and downs again, that I could not tell you a quarter of my history."

"When did you begin to steal first?"

"When I was a kid; I was sent errands by my mother, she gave me money to buy things for her, and I cheated her often, and a fellow that cheats his mother, you know, is rather a hopeful youth. But to tell you the truth I was partly spoiled by my mother, for she allowed me to do as I liked, and when I grew up I became acquainted with others like myself, and from prigging apples out of gardens I got to prigging pockets, and from that I got to be a 'screwsman' and a 'cracksman.' My first long sentence was seven years' transportation, and I never did a day's punishment hardly. In those days the 'legs' went on board ship at once, and were liberated or handed over to a master almost as soon as they arrived. Well, I completed my time, was two years a whaler, and went and settled in New Zealand, and that was the time I had most luck. I was a brick-maker, and made money as fast as I had a mind almost. I remained in New Zealand about fourteen years, and since I came home I have never had a day's luck; I went on the 'cross,' and got four years; after I had finished that bit, I went and lived with a 'moll' I knew, and spent all my money. When it was done I went out to look for work, and met with a young fellow who knew what sort of a 'bloke' I was, so he says ' You are just the fellow I want, Bill; my master goes to the bank to-morrow morning, and draws the wages money, after he draws it he puts it in a drawer in his desk, and then goes out for about an hour, and leaves the office without anyone in it. I have got two keys for the door and the desk, but as I would be found out if I attempted to take the cash, I will give you the keys, and we will divide the spoil. As soon as the way is clear I will hang out a handkerchief and then you will know that all is right.' Well I took the keys, and went to the factory at the hour named, I waited some little time, and at last I saw the signal agreed upon. Up I goes to the door, as if I had a right to the place, marched boldly into the office, and before you could say 'Jack Robinson' I had the bag full of cash. Well, off I bolts to my lodging, changed my clothes, and counts nearly one hundred pounds. I got the half, as arranged, and never wrought a day's work till all was spent—I spent about one pound per day. After that I took to hawking, and I might have made a living at it but I got drunk, did a place over, and got caught in the act, and here I am."

"How many robberies may you have committed ?"

"Goodness knows ! with the exception of the time I was in New Zealand I've been always on the 'cross.'"

"What was the largest you ever got ?"

"Five hundred pounds."

"I understand, most of these large robberies are 'put up' jobs, like the one you have mentioned ?"

"Yes, most of them are; the risk would be too great if that was not the case."

"Have you ever been flogged ?"

"Yes, severely."

"How did you like it ?"

"Like it ! why not at all, of course ; who would like a flogging ?"

"Would the chance of getting another flogging not deter you from committing another crime ?"

"I would as soon be 'topt' as be flogged now, because a good bashing would kill me ; but no fear of punishment would deter me, if I saw my way clear to get off. I never do a job until I feel certain I'll escape. If I'm caught that's my fault, and I must chance the punishment, whatever it may be.

Another 'legging' would kill me, but if I cannot get a living at hawking I will be forced to go on the 'cross,' and 'God help the man that tries to catch me.' These places are getting so hot that a fellow had better commit murder and be 'topt' at once."

"If you had a safe where would you place it to be most secure ?"

"In the street, and then your servants couldn't put you away."

"How would you carry your gold watch if you had one ?"

"Well, I would have one with a patent bow, and I would take care not to flash my chain. If you keep your chain out of sight you are pretty safe as long as you are sober, and every man who gets drunk ought to lose his watch ; the thief should get a reward for doing that job. It's safer of course to carry the watch in the fob than in the waistcoat pocket, particularly if the chain is exposed, but it can easily be taken from any part, if the chain is seen, unless you have a catch in your pocket to hold it. You know the way we do is to twist the bow of the watch and it breaks in a second."

"What do you get for a watch, usually ?"

"From three to six pounds, according to the value of the watch."

"That seems a very low price to get for a good gold watch ?"

"Yes, but five pounds, I assure you, is considered a good price by the man who stands 'fence,' and if a fellow can get eight or ten in a day he may do very well at that, but I have not done any 'buzzing' for a long time, I am too old for that game, and I can't afford to run a risk for five pounds. This hot work in prison will make thieves look after larger stakes."

"I would recommend you very strongly to go on the square when you get out, and not on the cross; you might easily make a better living by hawking than at this weary work, at all events."

"I mean to go on the square as long as I can do without working, I am not able for hard work and I do not intend to do any more, neither in nor out of prison; but if I can't make a living honestly you may be sure I shall not starve."

CHAPTER XIX.

THE following are specimens of the conversations which take place among the prisoners as they meet in the ordinary course of their prison employment. They were quite unaware that there was anyone near listening to them, or taking more than an ordinary interest in their remarks to each other, and my report may be taken as a perfectly accurate representation of ordinary convict conversation and phraseology.

"Well, Dick, how are you?"

"Oh! pretty well, Ned, how's yourself?"

"Well, I'm among the middlings only. That beastly bad cheese they gave us yesterday hasn't agreed with me, and I think I shall hook it up to the 'farm'* for a week or two, and get a change of diet before going home. I am only waiting to get a bit of 'snout,' and then I shall send in a sick report. Have you heard what Larry and Tim have got this morning? Larry's got three days' bread and water, seven days' penal-class diet, and 'blued' fourteen days' remission; and Tim's got three days."

"Well, Larry partly deserves it. He was a fool to let the 'screw' see he had the 'snout;' but what was Tim's offence?"

"Speaking to a fellow in the ranks, and merely saying 'It was a fine morning;' he'll get turned out of the cook-house, too. It's a —— shame, when other fellows talk away in the ranks every day. I say, what day do you go home?"

"I ought to go on the 2nd, but these —— licenses will be late again, no doubt, and very likely I shall not go before the 10th or 20th of the month. Have you any message for me to carry out?"

"Do you remember 'Big Croppy?'"

"Yes."

"Well, he's been to my wife since he went out, and told her all manner of lies. He's told her that I accuse her of going with another man, and she has been to my mother and told her that she is not going to write to me any more, nor to live with me again. I have been to ask for a special sheet of paper to write

* Hospital.

and tell them that it is all lies Croppy has told them; but the —— governor won't grant me paper. So, as I am not due to write for nearly three months, I wish you would call on my mother and my wife, and tell them how things stand."

"I will, you may depend upon that, and I'll get some 'bloke' to give Croppy a pair of black eyes for his pains, the —— swine."

"Here comes Pat.—Well, Pat, have you heard that Larry and Tim have gone to chokey?"

"Yes," replied Pat; "but what screw reported Tim?"

"That leather-skinned cranky old terrier over there reported Tim, and the 'bloke' with the peg-top whiskers reported Larry."

"Bad'cess to the 'terrier!' I have a good mind to punch him in the ear-hole."

"That would fetch a bashing, Pat."

"Troth, and I've had a bashing once afore, and what I've had once I can do with agin."

"Did you holloa when you were bashed?"

"Holloa! by the piper, I sang out—

> 'The seeds of repentance, how can they take root,
> When I'm ruled by a tyrant and flogged like a brute;
> The plant of revenge is more likely to sprout
> When such monsters of jailers go strutting about.'

And I called them all the horrid names I could think on, and they were wild when they saw I was game."

" Where were you bashed ?"

" At Bermuda; and by the piper, they once flogged men before the altar there, and then called the prisoners into chapel and preached to them about forgiving one another, and showing mercy to one another, the —— hypocrites."

" What are you here for this time ?"

" Oh, nothing at all. I am like the bloke in the song—

> ' One day as I passed I looked into the kitchen,
> Where I saw a pot boiling, but not for poor Pat ;
> For love and for thieving I'd always an itchin',
> So I took out the mutton and put in the cat.'

" I understand there was a great many unnatural crimes committed at Bermuda ?"

" Oh ! shocking. The young lads would go about with their pockets full of money, and their hair decked up like girls. It was disgusting, 'pon my word; and do you know what the authorities called it when cases were brought before them ?"

" No."

" Why, ' malicious gambling.' That was to deceive the public, you know. There was plenty of ' snout' knocking about in all the prisons in those days, and a fellow hadn't to go a day without a taste as he has to do now sometimes. We used to have lots of rum at Bermuda, as well as ' snout,' and first-rate liquer, too. By the piper ! I wish I had a drop now."

" How much could you do with ?"

" A wee drop in a bucket, about two hoops up. The last time I'd a drop o' rum in me, do you know what I did ? I had on a very shabby coat, all torn at the elbows, and only one tail to it, so I spied a country bloke with his girl, dressed out in new toggery. I says to my pal, ' I say, O'Shockady, there's a new coat on that bloke's back that I must have on mine; he is just about my size. You go up and be messing about with his girl, and you'll see he will guard and offer to fight. You take off your coat and put up your ' props' to him, and get him to strip also. Well, I'll come up and see fair play, and while you're at the fists I'll leave my tog and take his, d'ye twig ?' Well, up O'Shockady went, and, my crikey ! if you had seen how the bloke fired up when his girl was insulted ! why, his coat was off in a jiffey, and it was soon farther off than he could catch, I can tell you. After I got round the corner O'Shockady gave in to the bloke and bolted, leaving him in his shirt-sleeves to escort the girl."

" That reminds me," said Dick, " of an affair I was once in. When I was a lad I ran away from home. I was afraid to go back, lest I should get a bashing. At that time there was a woman in the High Street of Edinburgh, who took in lads situated as I was, and made them go out and steal, to pay her for their lodging. There were about twenty of us in the house at the time I went; some of them wenches and some of them young chaps like myself. Well, one night we were rather hard up and we wanted a good feed, so five or six of us set out, along with a great stout fellow, and we actually stole a whole sheep that was hanging at a butcher's door, and the big chap swagged it home. The old woman had it put in the bed, and covered it with the bed-clothes, as if it was a sick person; and the 'bobbies' found it there before she had time to get it cooked for us, and, by jingo! we were all marched up to the 'lock-up' over it. Well, I got thirty days over that job. When I came out of jail I went to a fair in the neighbourhood, and I prigged a countryman's 'poke' as he was standing at one of those barrows where they shoot for nuts; and, by the piper! the 'copper' saw me and marched me off to the station. But just before coming out of the crowd I got twisted round a little behind the 'bobby,' and I passed the purse into his pocket. Well, off we marched to the station, and when we arrived there the policeman swore that I stole a purse, and that I had it on me, as he saw me put it into my pocket. They searched me, but of course found nothing, and I got off. Determined not to lose the 'poke,' which had a good many 'quids' in it, I watched the 'copper,' and prigged it out of his pocket again. It was the same 'bobby' as got me this bit, and I told him then all about it."

Q

"I once," chimed in Ned, "buzzed a woman on the 'fly,' and got her poke with eighteen bob in it; she soon missed it, and I saw her go into a shop, and watched her crying to the shopkeeper and telling him that she had got all her husband's earnings for the week stolen. Well, I knew she was a poor woman by that, and I went up and asked her if she had lost a purse, as I had found one. She said she had, and I gave it to her again. Now, mind you, I was very hard up at the time, but I don't hold with stealing from poor people. Men that have more than they know what to do with in a country where· thousands are starving, ought to have some of it taken from them : that I call 'fairation.' I once prigged a priest's pocket, and he collared me and said, 'Well, if you think you have a better right to that purse than I have, you may keep it.' 'Well, sir,' I said, 'I'm very hard up, and as there are only a few shillings in it I hope you will allow me to keep them,' and, by jingo ! if the good old fellow didn't let me off, blessings on his head for it. One of the narrowest escapes I ever had was one time I prigged a poke with only seven shillings and sixpence in it. The copper saw me, and chased me like Jehu. Well, I out with the money, pitched the purse away, so that it could not be easily got again ; and, one by one, I swallowed the coins, and just as I was getting the sixpence down my throat the 'bobby' had a hold

of me by the collar. Of course he was too late. I
hadn't a rap in my pockets, but it was very near a
'legging' for me. I had another narrow escape not
long before I got this bit. I knew a gentleman's
house where they laid out the breakfast dishes on
the table for an hour before they took breakfast.
During this hour the room was left untenanted, and the
window left open to let in the air. Well, I bolted in
and 'nicked' a nice silver teapot, cream jug, and one
or two other things, and off I started home, where I
'planted' the articles, and then went to bed. Shortly
afterwards a bobby came to the door, and although I
told them to say I was not at home, to get him kept
from coming in, by jingo! I soon found he was coming
to search the house. So I bolted out of bed like a shot,
put my clothes into a drawer, and up I went through
a sort of trap-door on to the roof of the house, and
perched myself behind the chimney of the next house,
with nothing on but my shirt and stockings; I hadn't
time even to get my trousers pulled on. Oh! didn't
I sit shivering there till they gave me the tip that
all was right in the house. The 'toff' that owned
the 'wedge' made a dreadful song about it next day,
and him wallowing in wealth, what do you think of
that? The copper knew I did that job, and had me
up on suspicion some time after, and gave me a drag
(three months) over it. The next bit I did was a
'sixer' (six months), and I escaped from prison in

about three weeks after I got it. Soon after that I got this seven 'stretch' (years), and, by the piper! I'll take care and not get the next for nothing!"

"Oh! crikey," cried Pat, "here's a new screw come; what has he been, I wonder?"

"Where is he?" said Ned.

"Yonder; he is coming this way, with a tall complexion, a leg o' mutton whisker, and a pock-marked shirt," replied Pat.

"Why, he's a big fellow?"

"Big! I should think he was. He is like a double-breasted beer barrel. He's been a screw at some other prison; you can see that by the cut of his jib."

"Oh! I know him," said Dick, "he's from Dartmoor; he is not a bad sort of fellow, that. He is straightforward, and if ever he takes a prisoner before the governor he speaks the truth, and you know they don't all do that, by a long way."

"How long were you at the Moor, Dick?"

"Three years; but it's not like the same place now. Oh! we had rare sport there at one time. There was an old half 'barmey' chap when I was there, who was once admitted to the 'communion,' and it happened to be his turn to get the wine first, and, by the piper! if he didn't drink every drop that was in the cup, and cried, 'Oh! that's fine! I do love this! I do love this!' We had

plum pudding at Christmas in those days, and the
roughs did anything they liked almost, if they
didn't strike a screw. There was too much license
there then, but now it's all the other way. What
good is this humbugging system going to do us?
If they want to keep us out of prison why don't
they get work for us that we can earn a proper
living at?"

" Oh! they're a lot of jackasses, that's what they
are; they don't know what to do with us," said Ned.

" Look at this classification, and these marks and
badges," said Dick, " why, isn't it scandalous the way
the public are gulled? First there were big leather
badges, that would cost probably a thousand pounds
at all the prisons. Then these were done away with,
and we had badges half the size, and then, after a
few weeks, these were replaced by bits of cloth. I
wonder what they mean by all these changes of
dress? Do they think it punishes us?"

" No doubt they do."

" What fools they must be; what do we care what
we wear in prison, as long as it isn't thin rags that
won't keep out the cold. Oh, have you read that
article in one of the periodicals about the Andaman
Islands?"

" No."

" Well, the bloke who writes it proposes to send
convicts out there, and keep them for life and compel

them to marry prostitutes or female convicts, and
then when the 'kids' are grown to take them away
from them ! The fool ! why, all convicts haven't life
sentences, and does he think that they would remain
out there and do as he liked after their time was
up ? It isn't likely."

" Why, that would be worse than the slave trade,"
said Ned, "and wouldn't there be a nice crop of
murders there ? Why, they would require to get a
factory specially for making hemp ropes to hang the
culprits."

" Who is it that writes the article ?" asked Pat.

" A government commissioner, but he does not
give his name."

" Troth, and I should be ashamed to give it if I
was he ; I propose he should be taken and compelled
to marry a 'tail,'* and sent out to try it himself
first; why such men are not fit to live, and these
are Christians ! those are the men who do unto
others as they wish to be done by, God help us ?"

" Have you heard what the director did when he
was down on Saturday ?" enquired Ned.

"A precious sight of good he does to be sure,"
replied Dick, "why he has given orders that no
prisoner is to be allowed to see him about the food
and the marks, and you must tell the chief warder
what you want to see the director about before you

* Prostitute.

can be allowed to go before him. Isn't that a pretty
thing ? What a nice easy way of earning a thousand
a year the director has ?"

" What has caused this fresh order ?"

" There were two causes—three of the convalescent
invalids went to the director to ask to be able-bodied
in order to get the able-bodied diet. They are doing
as much work now, except that they are not quite so
long at it, but they are willing to work for the diet
the same as the others. The director refused to allow
them to work more, and of course they can't get the
grub, and he gave orders that no more of such
cases should be allowed to come before him.
Another case was this—two fellows saved their
cheese on the sly for several weeks, and in this way
managed to have each about four cheeses beside
them. Well, one of them told the officials what he
was going to do, and the other kept his intentions
secret. The first one went before the director and
asked him if he would be kind enough to look at
the cheese he had been supplied with for some
weeks, and see whether it was the quality it ought
to have been. The governor chimed in at once, and
said that this was the only complaint he had heard
about the cheese, and that all the other prisoners
were satisfied. The prisoner was then bounced out
of the room, and threatened with a 'report' if he
complained again. Well the next man was called,

and this happened to be the other 'bloke' with the four cheeses. Before going in he took them out of his pocket, and what do you think they did ? Why, he wasn't allowed to go before the director at all; they squared him and coaxed him, and at last persuaded him not to insist on seeing the director at all, by threatening to send him to the refractory cells for having four cheeses on his person, which was quite contrary to the prison rules ! Isn't it a —— shame the way the head blokes go on ? How can they expect a fellow to reform when they rob us of our food and show us a bad example ?"

"What o'clock is it, Pat; d'ye see the clock there ?"

" It wants a quarter to three ; I say, Dick, will you give me a mutton for a pudding, that beastly stuff lays heavy on my stomach, and I know you are fond of it."

" I don't mind, but how are you to get it sent to me ?"

" I'll send it by some fellow in our ward who works in your gang."

" I am hard up for snout," said Ned, " can you give us a bit, Pat ? Upon my word I've just had one old pipe head for the last three days and it wasn't up to much, it had been too much used."

" Well, I'll lend you an inch or two, but I hope you will soon pay me back; why there is none to be had now under a bob an ounce ; but I say, Ned, if you should get another legging I would advise you to declare yourself a Jew. You look something like a sheeney at any rate. Why look at that old 'Chick-arlico;' he goes twice a week to school and has two Sundays every week, besides ever so many feast days."

" Oh, I can do another 'bit,' no matter whether I am Jew, Turk, or Christian ; but if I get an easy job I mean to go on the square, upon my word I do."

" Who'll employ you, do you think ?"

" Why, I shall go to the society."

" The society be —— ! they will not do you any good."

" I believe it is under new management now, and they don't cheat a fellow out of his gratuity as they used to do ; but I think it's a wrong name to give it —The Prisoners' Aid Society! the very cases requiring most aid they won't assist at all, and unless a fellow is stout and hearty and has got some gratuity they won't have anything to do with him. If I had only a few shillings coming due to me they would not aid me, but as I have five or six pounds they will, now that looks suspicious. Then, if I had lost a leg, like that bloke over there, they wouldn't aid me. But if I don't go to the society I will, perhaps, go to Ireland and give them a turn there."

" Oh !" said Pat, "you'll find nothing that wants lifting there."

" Have you been to Spike Island, Pat ?"

" Yes."

" What sort of place is it, and what about this Irish system ?"

" Oh ! the place is something like the public works here, and as for the Irish System—I can see nothing in it except that they get most of the prisoners sent to America, and if they would send *us* there, we might get a living too, without going on the cross ! There are not many regular prigs in the Irish prisons. Many of them are fellows who got into trouble in some drunken row, and the people in Ireland are not so prejudiced against convicts as the English are, so that work is easier got; another thing is when your time is near up you are trusted a little, and get some liberty to go about. In this way the authorities can see who's who. Then the numbers are fewer altogether, and a small lot of men are easier dealt with, you know, than many thousands. It wouldn't work quite so well here, but the great thing is sending the prisoners abroad in some way or other. Do you know that Lafferty and Badger are going to be sent to New Orleans, by the Catholic Aid Society ?"

" No! what will Lafferty do there ?"

" Oh ! he must go on the cross, I expect, but Badger is able to work. He's a very good 'buzzer,' is Lafferty, mind you, and he might do very well out there."

"Well, the time's up Ned, I suppose you'll be going up to the 'farm' to night, and we sha'n't see you again. Well, old fellow, take care of old Tommy's black draughts, and look after yourself when you get out. Good-bye."

"Good-bye, old fellow, good luck to ye."

"Fall in."

"There's the officer shouting 'fall in.'"

"Well, ta; ta."

"Ta ta."

CHAPTER XX

DURING the last year of my imprisonment a bill relating to the crimes of murder and man-slaughter was brought before Parliament, and the discussion in the House of Commons which ensued was much commented upon by the prisoners. About the same time I read a lecture touching on the same subject, which had been delivered to the Young Men's Christian Association, at Exeter Hall, and it may not be out of place here if I venture to express my opinion on the subject as well, possessing as I do the advantage over most of those who have discussed it out of doors, in having heard the opinions of those likely to commit such crimes, and having a familiar acquaintance with their habits, and the motives from which they act. The reverend lecturer to whom I have referred, based his argument for the continued infliction of capital punishment on the perpetual obligation of the Mosaic law : " Whoso sheddeth man's blood, by man shall his blood be shed." He also maintained, if I understand him rightly, that the office of the hangman ought to be considered the highest object of human ambition, and that the hangman himself should take precedence of archbishops, kings, and emperors, inasmuch as he occupied the position of Almighty God, taking vengeance for the shedding of human blood. I confess I can scarcely conceive of a Christian man occupying such a position, neither can I agree with the reverend lecturer that the command given to Noah was intended to extend to all generations and societies of men. When it was promulgated there were only a few individuals left to people the universe, and the command was made *absolute.* There is no intimation of any distinction between the deliberate and the accidental shedding of human blood, and until some such distinction is made our conceptions of the eternal rectitude and justice of God, must be of a very peculiar and imperfect kind. That some distinction ought to be made is a fact which men in all ages and of all degrees of civilization have recognized, and have found their authority for making such a distinction, not in any spoken or written law, but in a much higher and older law than these, the universal conscience of mankind. That such a distinction was found necessary as the race became more numerous, is conclusively shown by the promulgation of the Mosaic law : "He that smiteth a man so that

he die shall be surely put to death, and if a man lie
not in wait, but God deliver him into his hand, then
I will appoint thee a place whither he shall flee."
(Ex. xxi., 12, 13.)   This was a great modification of
the original injunction, and also shows clearly, to my
mind at least, that all human punishments should be
regulated by the condition of the people for whose
benefit they are designed.   Again, in the same chapter
from which I have already quoted, I find the following, "Thou shalt give life for life, eye for eye, tooth
for tooth, hand for hand, foot for foot, &c.," a law
evidently designed for a semi-barbarous people, and
admitting of prompt administration and summary
execution.   Turning to the Christian law on the subject we find, " Ye have heard that it hath been said
an eye for an eye, and a tooth for a tooth, *but I* say
unto you that ye resist not evil."   This would appear
to introduce a new principle of forbearance, and if
we refer to the case of the woman taken in adultery,
where the legal penalty was death, we find that
mercy, and not vengeance, is the principle on which
our penal code ought to be based.

But leaving scriptural grounds and descending to
those of expediency merely.   Does capital punishment
deter men from committing murder more effectually
than perpetual imprisonment would ?   I believe that
999 out of every 1000 of our convicts even would
not commit deliberate murder, although the penalty

was only a few months' imprisonment and detection *certain*, unless under peculiar temptation or provocation. It is a crime naturally abhorrent even to the thief, and the majority of those men capable of committing wilful murder would on the whole, I believe, prefer to be hanged out of their misery, than remain in prison all their life. If all hope of release could be utterly extinguished, very few of such men would chance perpetual imprisonment, if they had it in their option. Of course we could not banish hope from the minds of all, and therefore many would at first cling to life, and after a few years seek death as a release from bondage, and even commit suicide rather than endure such suffering longer. I knew one prisoner who pleaded to be hanged, and others who would certainly prefer execution if they had no hope of ultimate liberty. The general opinion of those who had been in prison ten or twelve years out of a 'life' sentence was in favour of execution at once, as being the less dreadful alternative, so that with respect to punishment as a deterring influence, I have no doubt that perpetual imprisonment would be more efficacious than the capital sentence.

Those who are capable of deliberately taking human life with the view of obtaining money, may be divided into two classes. The one class comprising such as prisoners who perpetrate the crime cunningly and in secret, in the firm belief that they

will escape detection; the other class are the high-
waymen and garotters, who go daringly and violently
to work, pretty sure in their own minds that they
will be clever enough to escape.

With regard to the former class, the deterring influence is detection. Capital sentence, perpetual imprisonment, or even a less severe sentence would
operate equally in preventing the commission of the
crime in their case, because the idea is not generally
present in their mind when they premeditate it, or
is completely outweighed by the fear of detection
or discovery. With reference to the second and
bolder class, a lingering imprisonment would appear
more horrible in their estimation, and exercise an
equal if not a greater deterring influence than the
scaffold. Some of those men with whom I have met
would glory in dying 'game' as they term it. Those
who commit murder in order to gratify feelings of
revenge, usually, I believe, find the gratification of the
passion so sweet that they are for the time quite
regardless of their own lives; and when jealousy is
the cause of murder, it often happens that the
murderer takes the law into his own hands and
visits upon himself the penalty. I met cases in point,
and in none of them did the fear of the death sentence
operate against the perpetration of crime. They had
made up their minds to lose their lives, and did not
calculate on escape. Such cases are not common,

however, and perhaps it is not possible to prevent them occurring.

Those murders perpetrated for the love of money might to some extent be prevented by the general elevation of the mass of society, and by increasing the swiftness and certainty of detection; and I have come, after long study of the subject, and from frequent contact with those saved from the gallows, to the conclusion that capital punishment may now be safely abolished in this country. In all countries where secondary punishments are severe and capital punishments rigorously inflicted, murders are numerous, and in countries where the machinery for the detection of crime is defective it may be the same. Earl Russell, in a late edition of his work on the constitution, expresses opinions on this subject with which I coincide, but I disagree with him when he prescribes imprisonment and hard labour as being the most suitable method of dealing with criminals not capitally punished; I refer, of course, to imprisonment and hard labour as generally understood.

There are three systems of imprisonment: the solitary, the separate and silent, and the promiscuous association of all prisoners at the public works.

The solitary system feeds the lunatic asylums, the separate system has its advantages, if not too long continued, and of the promiscuous association system I have already at some length given my opinion.

R

In my humble estimation a prison ought to be a place for extracting as much usefulness as possible out of a prisoner for the benefit of that society whose laws he has offended; but the "hard labour" in our prisons is not useful in any sense of the word, either to the prisoner or society, it is sheer waste of energy, which is in itself an evil, and it gives the prisoner an aversion to labour of all kinds, which is another and a much greater evil. Moreover, long imprisonments are injurious to the prisoner under any discipline. If you take a bird, and place it in a cage, and next day liberate it, it will ever retain a dread of confinement; but, if you keep it in a prison for years, and then open the cage door, instead of the sudden eager flight to freedom, it will hover round its little prison, perhaps it will even re-enter it, preferring it to that liberty which it has lost the power to enjoy. So it is with many prisoners, keep them confined, and accustom them for years to prison life, such as it is in the most approved "models," or indeed under any conceivable mode of discipline consistent with unshortened life in such a place, and they will re-enter the world in a great measure, unfitted for the business of life.

I remember having a conversation with an intelligent prisoner who was by no means a criminal at heart. He asked me what means would I recommend for the destruction of these schools of crime?—for so he called the convict prisons.

"Sentence Charles Dickens to ten years' penal servitude, and allow him to use his pen," I replied.

" Well," he said, " I daresay that might do, especially if those intended for our future judges were sentenced along with him ; but why should we not try to enlighten the public when we are liberated ?"

" You might do so," I replied, "and I sincerely hope you will do so ; but I fear, like the down of a thistle on an elephant's back, so would the words of a convict fall upon the public ear !"

" Look at Napoleon III.," said my friend, "he is an ex-convict, and do his words fall lightly on the public ear ?"

" His is hardly a case in point," I said ; "the greater the criminal, or rather the higher the object he endeavours unlawfully to obtain, the less prejudiced is society against him. They regard these Fenians for instance in a different light to us, yet these men at bottom are or would be wholesale destroyers of human life, whilst we had no intention of doing anyone any injury either in person or property. We are loyal, they are traitors. We would willingly lay down our lives to regain our lost characters and attain to an honourable and useful position in society; they will go out of prison rebels, ready to take up arms against all authority save that of their misguided chiefs, whenever they can do so with apparent safety ! Yet these men will be more favourably received by society than you or I will be. You will find when you get free that your position will be very different from what it was, and that anything you say will be viewed with suspicion, as coming from a prejudiced and untrustworthy person, and a well-told falsehood by an official will far outweigh the whole truth if related by a prisoner."

" I could now prove," said my friend, " by the Blue Books, that most of the reports sent to the Home Office regarding these establishments are unreliable, and calculated to deceive and mislead the public as well as the government."

" You will require to be very guarded," I replied ; " and above all things adhere strictly to the truth, and if you can gain the ear of some eminent man who takes an interest in the question, you might be the means of doing your country much service."

In consequence of such conversations as the one I have just related, I was led to form the idea of giving this narrative to the public. If it should lead to any change or modification in our criminal law, conducive to the welfare and security of society, I shall consider that my labours have not been altogether vain and unprofitable.

A change of government having taken place during the last year of my imprisonment I had the good fortune to get a few months' more remission of sentence than might otherwise have been the case.

While I feel truly thankful to those noblemen and gentlemen and other friends who interceded for me, my special gratitude is due to Mr. Walpole, for the promptitude he displayed in acknowledging my claim to the few months' mitigation of punishment it was in his power to bestow.

On a Friday morning I was unexpectedly called before the governor, and informed that my license had arrived. I was asked certain particulars in reference to my future intentions and address. I was next measured for a shoe, the only decent and honest article of clothing I ever received in prison ; tried on a suit of clothes, and had my portrait taken. On the Saturday morning I was weighed and measured, and taken before the chaplain to receive a few formal words of parting advice. On the following Monday I was again taken before the governor to hear my license read. On Tuesday morning I was removed to Millbank Prison, and lodged there for the night, in a cell along with two other prisoners going to liberty like myself. We slept on narrow dirty mattresses, laid on the floor, so close as to be touching each other. One of my new companions had been nearly four years in the lunatic asylum at Fisherton, and had recovered. The other was a young professional thief, belonging to London, whose mind was just on the verge of insanity, through long confinement in separate cells. To sleep on the floor of a dusty cell,

between two such companions, was not quite so comfortable as a bed in the Hotel Meurice, at Paris,
where I had spent my last free night. Every
moment that divided me from the hour of my liberation now seemed magnified into days. Wednesday
morning at last dawned upon me. I was taken out
and placed before a regiment of policemen, who each
scrutinized me, and that done I received my license.
With feelings of inexpressible thankfulness and
gratitude to God I heard the heavy prison doors
close behind me, and once more I inhaled the sweet
free air of Heaven!

Tears streamed down my cheeks as I trudged
along the streets, in my shabby clothes and with my
deal crutch. I felt a new punishment creeping over
me, even whilst the glorious sun of freedom was
shedding its welcome rays on my dishonoured head.

With nineteen shillings and threepence in my
pocket, but with my reputation lost, my health
ruined, alone and a cripple, whom no " Prisoners' Aid
Society" would assist, I was expected to begin anew
the battle of life!

While I write these lines the bitterness of my new
punishment has already visited me. Repulsed from
every door where I seek employment, waiting
patiently for the replies to my applications for advertised situations, which never come, the brand of the
convict has indeed become the very mark of Cain,

and I feel as if my fellowmen shrink from me as they pass. Fortunately I found at the post-office a few pounds sent to me from my brother, which, with slight additions, have enabled me to procure a mechanical leg, and to live till I have completed this narrative. But what is the fate of the many so situated, with no friends to help them, save the workhouse or the prison once again? A dreary life amongst paupers, or a short life of pleasure and crime, and long years of bondage to atone for it. Do you wonder if some choose the latter? . . . . May you, gentle reader, never know what it is to lose your limb, your liberty, your character, or your home. May my history prove a beacon to warn you from the quicksands of ambition, on which so many human souls are wrecked, and may your little barque, wafted by gentle sunny gales, be safely steered across the great ocean of life, and at last be securely moored in that haven where blessedness and peace for ever reign!

APPENDIX.

APPENDIX.

————

Consultat Général de France en Angleterre.

Londres, le 1er September, 1863.

Le Consul Général de France a Londres a l'honneur de transmettre á Monsieur ————, avec prière de vouloir bien lui en accuser réception, une lettre et une médaille qui lui sont destinées.

Monsieur ————, *Negociant.*

Ministere de l'Agriculture du Commerce, et des Travaux Public—Secrétarian Général, Mèdaille.

Paris, le 22 Juin, 1863.

Monsieur à la suite du traité de commerce conclu le 23 Janvier, 1860, entre la France et la Grande Bretagne, le Gouvernement de Sa Majesté l'Empereur a du procéder à une enquète dont les résultats devaient le mettre à même de determiner les Tarifs des droit d'importation en France des produits fabriqués en Angleterre. Pour Consacrer le Souvenir de cette enquête, l'une des plus importantes de ce genre qui aient été faites en France, le Gouvernement à fait frapper une médaille commemorative et il a décidé qu'un exemplaire en bronze de cette médaille serait mis à la disposition des Industriels qui ont déposé dans l'enquéte. J'ai l'honneur, Monsieur, de vous adresser à ce titre l'exemplaire qui vous est destiné. Recevez, Monsieur, l'assurance de ma consideration tres distinguée.

Le Ministre de l'Agriculture, du Commerce et des Travaux Public,

G. ROUHER.

Monsieur ————, *Negociant.*

[It is requested that any further communication
on the subject be addressed to the Secretary to
the Board of Trade, Whitehall, London, S.W.]

Office of Committee of Privy Council for Trade,

Whitehall, 9th May, 1861.

SIR,

I am directed by the Lords of the Committee
of Privy Council for Trade to transmit to you the
accompanying Volume, which contains the evidence taken
by the Counseil Supérieur du Commerce on the Industries
of England and France, during their recent enquiry at
Paris, in connection with the Commercial Treaty between
the two countries. In requesting your acceptance of this
Work, of which a limited number of Copies has been
placed at the disposal of Her Majesty's Government by
the Government of France, I am to convey to you the
best thanks of this Board for the valuable assistance
which you rendered upon that occasion, both to the
Counseil Supérieur and to the British Commissions.

I am, Sir,

Your obedient Servant,

J. EMMERSON TENNENT.

Order of License to a Convict, made under the Statutes 16 & 17 *Vic., c.* 99, *s.* 9; *and* 27 & 28 *Vic., c.* 47, *s.* 4.

Whitehall,   day of   18

Her Majesty is graciously pleased to grant to

who was convicted of   at the

on the   day of   18   , and was then

and there sentenced to be kept in penal servitude for the

term of   , and is now confined in the

Her Royal License to be at large from the day of his liberation under this order, during the remaining portion of his said term of penal servitude, unless the said

shall, before the expiration of the said term, be convicted of some indictable offence within the United Kingdom, in which case such License will be immediately forfeited by law, or unless it shall please Her Majesty sooner to revoke or alter such License.

This License is given subject to the conditions endorsed upon the same, upon the breach of any of which it shall be liable to be revoked, whether such breach is followed by a conviction or not. And Her Majesty hereby orders that the said   be set at liberty within Thirty days from the date of this order.

Given under my hand and seal.

Signed,   S. H. WALPOLE.

True Copy ⎱   E. Y. W. HENDERSON,
License to be at large. ⎰ Chairman of the Directors of Convict Prisons.

CONDITIONS.

1.—The holder shall preserve his License, and produce it when called upon to do so by a Magistrate or Police Officer.

2.—He shall abstain from any violation of the law.

3.—He shall not habitually associate with notoriously bad characters, such as reputed thieves and prostitutes.

4.—He shall not lead an idle or dissolute life, without visible means of obtaining an honest livelihood.

If his License is forfeited or revoked in consequence of a Conviction for any Offence, he will be liable to undergo a term of Penal Servitude equal to the portion of his term of   years which remained unexpired when his License was granted, *viz.:*—the term of two years and eleven months.

NOTICE.

He shall report himself to the Police on discharge, and subsequently once in each month; and if he changes his residence from one Police District to another, he shall report himself to the Police of the locality he leaves, and to the Police of that to which he goes, within three days of his arrival: if he fails to do so, his License will be forfeited.

In the foregoing " Ticket-of-leave" the word Licence is spelt with an *s.* In the Police Documents it is spelt with a *c.*—So much for the education of Government Officials.

SAVOY STEAM PRESS, SAVOY STREET, STRAND.

www.ingramcontent.com/pod-product-compliance
Lightning Source LLC
Chambersburg PA
CBHW030731280326
41926CB00086B/1136